Geneva Two

By

Russell B. Smith

✠ ✠ ✠

Geneva Two

ISBN-13: 978-1500697464

About this project

To be clear, Geneva Two does not exist. It is a fiction, a mental exercise, a utopia in the classic sense of "no place." None of these people exist, except in the odd crannies of my mind. Nor do any of these characters represent anyone living, dead, or living-dead.

I even invented a persona to take on the role of the narrator/interviewer: Hatcher Christolphson. In early drafts, Hatcher struggled to wedge his story into this book. He clamored for his voice, a distinctive voice that speaks from a outlook different than mine, to have more chapters. He dumped his backstory across my worktable and begged for a few paragraphs more.

Alas, this book isn't about Hatcher.

I set out to write a utopia. An unfortunate choice of genre, I know; most utopias are stiff Potemkin villages filled with pleasantly dull characters. When was the last time you found yourself tearing through Thomas More's *Utopia*, eager to see what happened next? Did Francis Bacon's *New Atlantis* keep you up into the wee hours of the morning? Have you even heard of *City of the Sun*? Don't feel bad – nobody reads this stuff except academics, pundits, and other assorted lunatics.

Of the lot, B.F. Skinner's *Walden Two* rises on the horizon as a literary oasis. Where other utopias trot out Stepford-like mouthpieces for their authors' ideals, Skinner's characters had spit in their mouths and blood in their veins. They wrestled with the practical outworkings of a community built upon the foundation of Behavioral Psychology. In their struggles, they took on a depth, a texture, a maturity that I've not found in the characters of other utopias. These characters made the Walden

Two community tangible, as though I might find it nestled in the rolling hills 20 minutes outside the city limits. That scientist Skinner worked more powerful magic than all those Renaissance philosophers.

Skinner haunted me. If this winsome atheist could pull off a readable utopia, shouldn't someone in the Christian community be able to write something comparable?

And so I tried. I set out to write a Christian utopia.

And I failed.

No matter how hard I worked at it, I couldn't write one. The essence of utopian literature, as near as I can tell, is to envision the proper ordering of society to maximize happiness in a self-perpetuating system. Utopias paint pictures of tidiness and perfection: the people are agreeable; the trains run on time. All works well, and everybody is content.

I couldn't do it. It would be a lie.

Humans don't submit well to perfection, at least not in this mortal coil. We are, each of us, marred. Stained. Tainted. We all must admit, if we are honest, to the stream of selfishness within. Pull the right lever and this stream swells into a raging unstoppable river.

This selfishness is, at its fountainhead, rebellion. Rebellion, ultimately, against God.

We call this "sin."

Most people think this word is a joke, a word on par with "naughtiness."

No. Sin is deadly serious. And it infects us.

And I'm afraid I'm just not smart enough to write a vision of a society in which sin is perfectly corralled. I'm too mired in the mess myself. That's where Hatcher came in handy.

You see Hatcher is a reporter. He's jaded and cynical. He has faced sin and seen the thousand or more guises that it wears.

I decided to sic Hatcher on my little non-utopia. He would interview the people of Geneva Two and give a kind of oral history of the place. Hatcher's job was to make this book less B.F. Skinner and more Studs Terkel. Instead of structure, Hatcher would keep the focus on stories. Little stories, vignettes. And if Hatcher did his job, then those stories would be honest, earthy, real. Very un-utopia.

Hatcher and I found that some of the people of Geneva Two are vain and insufferable. Others are downright irritating. They contradict one another. As the interviews began to coalesce into a mosaic depicting this community, Hatcher's journalistic integrity demanded that we be fair even to those characters with whom I disagree. We would have no straw men here.

And among these people, we found grace. We found both fracturing and healing. We found idealism and arrogance, tenderness and toughness, wisdom and folly. Yet permeating it all was grace and transcendence and trust in the living God who is every bit a part of this community. The thing that unites these characters is that they look to God: God who saves, God who calls, God who sends. We found that the stories did not end with stain, rebellion, and sin. The stories, each in their own way, pointed to God.

But enough of my introduction. Let me give Hatcher his moment in the sun, as he introduces to us the community of Geneva Two....

Soli Deo Gloria
Russell Smith
Cincinnati, OH
December 2014

Introduction

A plate of pecan pie, offered by a gleaming-eyed matron, first clued me in to the difference of this place. I've accepted *kule naa-ilanga* from a Maasai villager. I've sipped coffee hand-ground and slow-roasted by an Eritrean hostess. I've sat on eye-jarring colored carpets with stone-faced Andean dwellers who offered me unspeakably foul concoctions of fermented coca leaf and human saliva. I might also mention that I've enjoyed my fair share of pecan pie. Even so, I was struck that this moment was distinctive.

The members of the Geneva Two community had invited me to their monthly community potluck. It was a pleasant Midwestern summer evening. The aroma of smoldering charcoal wafted from the Edmonds' yard, where tables groaned under the colorful assortment of food: corn cobs roasted in their light green sheaves, bright red garden-fresh tomatoes, a giant bowl of fresh-picked blackberries (several purple-lipped children ran about, for the picking had also involved snacking), orange cantaloupe, yellow squash casserole, and fresh cut watermelon glistening in the evening sun. There was also an assortment of salads: German potato salad, Asian wonton salad, spinach salad with strawberries and Vidalia onions. Of course no cookout is complete without the meats: cured country ham with biscuits, grilled bräts and burgers, homemade fried chicken, to name a few. Easily, there was enough food to feed the 80 or 90 people mingling on the lawns along both sides of Onieda Street.

A gathering of elderly people perched in camping chairs under the shade of a large oak tree. Children played a rule-morphing game of chase in the neighborhood park, a small, pine-tree-filled triangle defined by the odd layout of Oneida, Amana, and New Economy streets. A boisterous, laughing group of middle-aged men paid half-minded attention to the hodgepodge of grills under their supervision. Across the street, a twenty-something-year-old woman assembled s'mores for children clustered around a blazing fire pit. Dogs capered about; conversation percolated among a half-dozen knots of adults; a radio quietly played some upbeat pop-music, though the mélange of sounds made it hard to identify the artist or song.

This was a yard party, and yet it was different. These people were entirely comfortable in their own skins. I have attended many a yard party that vibrated with an unspoken urgency, an entertainment imperative, an anxious *need* to produce fun. The unspoken expectation was to labor at being louder, crazier, and cruder to prove that fun was indeed being had.

But these people had nothing to prove.

I have been to social chess matches in the guise of cocktail parties. Each invitee curated their personal brand through stylish wardrobes, polished gestures, and witty words; every public aspect of their person was weighed, studied, practiced, and performed. These parties were shopping excursions where everyone was selling or being sold.

But these people had nothing to sell.

I came here to find out who these people were. I came to learn how, in the middle of the greatest era of self-actualization this planet has ever seen, this group of people had chosen to live by the third world values of community, resource-sharing, and interdependence.

I can describe the physical events of the moment that plate of pecan pie slipped into my hand, but I'm still trying to figure out how to articulate my inner experience. My guard was up. My senses were alert for incongruity, for I knew that behind every Edenic façade lies a pit that reeks of Sheol. Every feel-good story has a shadow side, a darker tale behind it. I was sniffing for that story behind the story.

Yet, somehow in that moment, I felt my instinctive cynicism soften. Perhaps it sounds crazy, but I felt hope. I knew that I would find strife, dysfunction, and mess; no human community exists without those. Wherever two or three are gathered, there is conflict among them. Even so, I felt hope. Among these people, I sensed a readiness to acknowledge the darkness of life, but a refusal to give it the last word. I felt, for that moment, that all was well, and all manner of things were well.

Geneva Two is an intentional community. Such communities are nothing new. Any place people share a common locale and mutually agree upon rules for living, there you have intentionality. Think of a condo association: everyone lives in proximity and lives under certain rules. There you have a pale version of intentionality; the rules of a condo association focus mostly on maintenance of the building and grounds. Condo associations have rules about how to keep from driving each other crazy: no loud parties after ten o'clock, don't paint your porch gaudy colors, please don't change your car's oil in the driveway.

However the intentional community movement aims to create something more than a warren of civil individuals living in close quarters. Those drawn to intentional community seek to share the fullness of their lives together – the joys and pains, the tragedies and triumphs. Think medieval monasteries, hippie communes, and utopian settlements. Think about Shakers and Moravians and Pilgrim settlers. On the darker side you might remember Branch Davidians and Jonestown. Intentional communities are not all benign.

The Fellowship for Intentional Community (www.ic.org) estimates that there are over a thousand such communities in the

United States. These come in all shapes and varieties, some of them faith-based, others eco-centered, or oriented around a particular style of living. They sprout up in urban cores and in the farms of the heartland. Some take the shape of communes where the residents live in the same structure and share 100% of their income. Others develop as neighborhoods of private residences where the people agree to share resources. Whatever you say, good or bad, about intentional communities, it is likely true somewhere.

As I enjoyed the pecan pie, I gazed about at these people, this neighborhood. I savored being there among these social pioneers, these unsuspecting radicals. Theirs was the story I had come to tell, the story of Geneva Two.

Hatcher Christolphson
Correspondent for *American Eye Magazine*
September 2010

Evelyn Van Doehrn

Just around the corner from the main houses of the Geneva Two community is the well-kept home of Evelyn Van Doehrn. You can recognize it by the two flags framing the front porch steps: the American flag on the left; on the right, a banner with the green field and golden harp of Ireland. White wicker chairs with blue and beige floral print cushions give the front porch a comfortable, welcoming feel. Halfway up the brick walkway, I see that Mrs. Van Doehrn has laid out a traditional tea with crust-trimmed finger sandwiches. After we exchange pleasantries, she invites me to enjoy some refreshments. The cucumber and dressing are cool on my tongue and complement the bergamot of the Earl Grey tea in my delicate china cup.

Evelyn has lived in this neighborhood since 1952, when she and her husband Vernon married. After Vernon's untimely death in 1957, Evelyn went to work to support her two children. She maintained this home while the neighborhood transitioned from 1950s boom to 1970s stagnation and back to a renaissance of young families starting in the early 2000s. At age 85, Evelyn, back still straight and purpose still in her step, walks the neighborhood twice a day.

After exhaustive conversation about the old days in the neighborhood, we talk about her experience with the Geneva Two community.

I was speaking with Kyle Edmonds at the cookout. He tells me that you've been generous in sharing your knowledge of neighborhood history. He said it was 'a great blessing' learning from you.

Well that's very sweet of him. I'm glad that somebody is interested in the history. I've been here for a long time and I've seen neighbors come and go. They stay for a few years and then leave without ever getting to know what's here. That's just terrible, don't you think? There's heritage here that must be passed along. It made me sick that nobody was paying mind to all that was here.

Did you know that this neighborhood started as a frontier fort? Back in the early 1800s, when Cincinnati was a little river settlement nine miles away Colonel McFarland came here to set up a way station on the road to Columbus. He chose this site because it was a crossroads of old Indian trails – Montgomery Road and Overlook Road follow the paths of those same trails. Can you imagine? The roads we drive on were first blazed by Indians hiking through dense woods long since gone.

Well that's very interesting ...

Just a minute, young man, I've got more to tell you. You saw that old building up on the corner? Just as you turned on Overlook to come down to Onieda street? The building's a Comic Book shop now. But back in the late 1800's, it was a saloon and tavern – Annie Oakley used to visit there, coming in to sell wild game that she had shot. Of course that was before she was famous. History! There's so much history here, and it's all so important. Go up to that graveyard behind the Presbyterian Church and you'll find markers of Revolutionary War heroes. You'll see the graves of babies that died of smallpox. People lived here and loved this place and left their mark. If you sit still long enough, you can almost feel the weight of a thousand years of footsteps drumming by.

Here, dear, your plate is empty. Have another sandwich. No, no I insist, I made these, and I can't eat them all myself, so take a couple. Now where was I?

I was going to ask ...

Oh, Yes! History! It's so important, and it tells us who we are. But these young people don't care – they move in here, and then in two or three years they're gallivanting off someplace else. No roots, no time to learn about this place. They go chase their mansions out in these suburbs; or they run off to some other city that has more lights and sounds and bars. They can't be still and partake of what the good Lord put before their nose. It's very sad.

But things were different with the people of Geneva Two?

Oh, God love you, yes. Mind you, I don't understand all this "Geneva Two" business. To my mind they're just being neighbors – what neighbors ought to be, anyway. But these young people need to have their funny names and their internets, don't they? Well, it's all well for them.

I understand you had some difficulties with the Geneva Two people at first?

For the first time, Mrs. Van Doehrn pauses. I don't know what you mean. I've always gotten along fine with everyone in the neighborhood.

From what I've been told, you once ordered Nathan Probisco off your property and threatened to have him arrested.

Oh, that. That was ages ago. I didn't know Nathan very well, then. He felt pushy and aggressive to me, like he wanted to meddle in my affairs. Nobody likes pushy people, do they? I've always been an independent woman, and I don't cotton to anyone telling me what to do. I can take care of myself just fine, thank you.

I thought Nathan was a busybody, and I wasn't afraid to tell him so. Perhaps I had a little too much vinegar on my tongue when I spoke. It was only later that I found out how hurt he'd been; I still don't understand why – what would you say if someone started treating *you* like an old fossil? I do not need to be coddled, I tell you, and I will not put up with it.

For my part, I did apologize for yelling at him and threatening him. We're good friends, now.

I'm still not clear on what exactly the problem was. What was it that you thought he was being pushy about?

Listen, this is how it happened. When Nathan and Mathilde moved in, they invited the whole neighborhood by their house for a drop-in. I admit I was cautious. No one in the neighborhood had done anything like that for a long time. To tell you the truth, I thought it was some sales gimmick. I was sure that halfway through the party they were going to start selling PlastiWare or cleaning products or vitamin supplements. Don't pretend to like me just so you can sell me something – that makes me madder than a minister on Monday. Fortunately, that wasn't what they intended. It was a nice pleasant party and a chance to meet the neighbors. It felt a little like old times.

Well, I started to see a lot of the Probiscos – all of the Geneva people, really: the Klines, the Hoffeckers, the Edmonds, Alan Gasque. They would call or stop by to check on me. At first the attention was nice, but soon it felt like too much.

What made it too much?

Well, I'll tell you. Nathan kept asking if I needed help with anything – things around the house, yard work, and the like. Some of the others would do the same. I'm independent, so most of the time I said "no" – but they kept on bothering me.

Then one trash day I noticed that someone had brought my empty cans back from the street and put them beside my garage. In the mornings, I would find my newspaper on the doorstep rather than out in the walkway. Every so often, Mathilde would bring by soup – "Just because," she said. Those little things were nice, but I never asked for them.

Then, that winter, Nathan or somebody came by and shoveled my walkway every time it snowed. I didn't ask for it, mind you, they came over uninvited and did it. And I was grateful, but I'm not incapable of doing a little shoveling or hiring my own help.

Well, the pigs came to the stockyard in the spring. One Saturday the doorbell rang. When I opened the door there was Nathan standing on the porch with about five other young men grinning like idiots. They had brought lawnmowers, trowels, pruning shears and all kinds of other equipment. It looked like they were set to attack my entire landscape in one day.

I tell you, my kettle just boiled over – I felt like a charity project. I've kept this house in tip-top shape for forty years since Vernon died, and I've done it by myself. I raised two children and put them through college; I've taken care of myself, even after my children moved away. I am not someone's problem to be fixed. I don't need a handout so someone can feel better about himself. So, I yelled at Nathan to stop meddling in my life – to stop treating me like I'm a helpless old lady who didn't have sense enough to keep sugar in her cupboard.

And you said that you'd have him arrested for harassment if he or his friends ever came on your property again ...

Yes. Yes, that was a bit much, wasn't it? I shouldn't have done that. Vernon used to say that I was as subtle as a cyclone. That's the old Irish temper in me, I guess – when I was little, grandpa Malone called me his "little gingersnap" because I got so hot headed over things. It gets me into trouble sometimes. The words come out and then it's too late – there's blood and feathers on the ground.

What did Nathan do?

Nothing. His eyes went all watery, as though he were a scolded little boy about to cry. He didn't raise his voice. He quietly said, "Yes ma'am, I'm sorry to bother you."

When I closed the door I felt terrible. I brooded for days. I didn't know what to do – he was such a nice boy, and I had overdone it and hurt his feelings.

It's hard for people my age. Most of my friends are either dead or in nursing homes – I don't socialize with anyone that saw what I saw. I don't mean the big things like World War 2. It's everyday things that I miss talking about: boat trips to Coney Island; dancing when men and women held hands and had to know steps that didn't involve dirty moves. The full swell of an orchestra with horns and clarinets. Men wore proper suits and hats whenever they went out. Gentlemen held doors open for ladies. Where do you see that anymore? We felt safe when we walked around the neighborhood. Children spent their afternoons out of doors riding bikes, playing football, skipping rope, and enjoying themselves. Everyone watched the Ed Sullivan Show and the Ruth Lyons 50/50 Club.

Oh, I can talk about it, but you can't know what it was like unless you lived it. You just don't know what that world was and what has been lost. You young people love your computers and your cell phones and your overpriced coffee – but we had such goodness and wholesomeness when I was your age. And I don't have anyone around me who experienced it – they're all gone.

I read a story in the paper a few years back about an Eskimo woman in Alaska who was the last speaker of her tribe's language. Her children didn't want to learn the language. It was so sad, because when she died, her language would die with her. Not only her language, but her whole world. Her people had a way of seeing things that was theirs. There's wisdom in peculiar words and odd turns of phrase. This article said that some words summarized whole stories. She knew that when she died, all her people's way of talking about the world would be forgotten.

That's how I feel, sometimes. *We sit in silence for a while.* Anyway, I suppose I overreacted a bit to Nathan at first, but like I said, we get along fine now.

The years have taught me to trust my instincts. Though Mrs. Van Doehrn has shared some deep feelings about aging, I sense that she would rather not explore those feelings with further questioning. I return the conversation to her conflict with Nathan.

I see, but I'm still confused as to what is upsetting about people showing an interest in helping?

That's it. So many times, people come by and they only have an interest in helping – they don't have an interest in *me* or what I have to give them. They want to look after the little old lady who can't take care of herself. They want me to be their charity project while they make themselves feel good. You're not going to humiliate me so that you can feel like you've done your good deed for the day!

And that's how you felt about the Geneva Community?

At first, yes. It's not their fault, really. You get hit by a few of these do-gooders over the years and it makes you look a little more sharply at everyone else.

So what changed?

Nathan called and asked if we could talk. Just me and him. I invited him over for tea.

Naturally ...

He started by apologizing. He said he didn't mean to offend me in any way, and he wanted to make things right. And then he listened. I told him everything I just told you, and more. He didn't backtalk, he just listened.

When I was done, he asked if he could explain what he and his friends were up to. He showed me the Geneva Compact and explained about how they were creating a new kind of community. I told him that was very nice, but I wasn't interested in joining anything. Like I said earlier, I don't understand why they need this compact – just be neighborly like everyone is supposed to be and everything will be fine. But since no one else in the world seems to be acting like neighbors, I guess these Geneva people are off to a good start.

Nathan made it clear that he wasn't interested in my joining anything, but that they'd like to be friends. He asked if he could invite me to dinner from time to time – he wanted to hear some stories about what the neighborhood used to be like.

And everything was fine from then?

Not quite. I still felt like a mannequin in a store window around them. I declined a number of invitations. It took Lynn Chamblis to straighten me out. Gary and Lynn have been in the neighborhood a long time – not as long as I have, but a long time nonetheless – so, I know them and trust them.

Lynn took me to lunch and told me that she and Gary had been getting to know these young people and they thought they were bona fide. After that lunch, I planned a little tea party. I invited Gary and Lynn, the Probiscos, the Klines, the Hoffeckers, the Edmonds, Alan Gasque. None of us mentioned anything about my argument with Nathan. From that time on, we've been friends.

And what's it been like since?

It's interesting that Mathilde and I have drawn close. She was standoffish at first. But she used to work in the corporate world, and I understand her mind. She thinks in terms of projects, processes, and getting things done. When she heard me tell about how our neighborhood used to enter a float in the Baseball Opening Day Parade, she hatched an idea of doing it again – and she made me her chief advisor.

The children have come by and interviewed me for some of their school projects – they wanted to learn about local history, and I filled them up with a bushelful of stories. They tell me that they used what I told them to write articles for that internet encyclopedia.

Then there was the time the children were learning about World War 2. Jake Hoffecker came over and decorated my living room like a USO hall. The children dressed up in old clothes and we played Tommy Dorsey and Glenn Miller and Duke Ellington music. I told them stories about blackouts and the draft and women going to work in the factories. The kids loved it.

That was back before Alan Gasque and Jake had the falling-out – I tried to talk Jake into coming back – but that boy is stubborn. It's still awkward with them living around the corner, not being a part of the community anymore.

What other ways have you been involved with the Geneva Community.

Well, I let them help me with my yard – Kyle is so good with his garden. He and I have talked a little bit about what needs done. So he came up with an arrangement: he's teaching some of the teenage children how to do lawn and garden work. They use my yard as a learning laboratory. I insist on paying them of course. Kyle and I come up with the plan and then he hires the teenagers, just as though it were a real job. He does whatever he does with teaching them and checking up on their work. Then I pay him a flat fee, which covers supplies and payments for the children.

Nathan comes by from time to time and helps with minor household repairs – he always stays to chat – he doesn't pop in and out as though he were a handyman.

He's even got me coming to Bible study at Kyle's house – I don't care for the guitar and the modern songs – but Kyle is a good teacher. He's helped me understand more about the Bible than I ever learned in church before.

It feels like the old days again. These Geneva folks do different things. But the spirit they bring to what they do makes it feel a little bit like it was before.

Mathilde Probisco

I meet Mathilde Probisco at Ground Up Coffee shop, just five minutes away from the Geneva Two community.   The shop is nestled in the neighborhood's business district, sharing the street with stores like Herr Drummer Hoff Used Books, Far Far Away Vintage Toy Mall, and the Menschhaus Gastropub.

Mathilde, a competitive runner and triathlete, is tall, lean, and muscular.   With her wavy blonde hair spilling behind her shoulders, she might be a Valkyrie of old, neatly attired in modern blue jeans and a red button-down shirt.   Mathilde worked for several years as a banking industry systems analyst, but now stays at home, investing her best time and energy in her children's development.   I find her surprisingly youthful and energetic for a woman who has four children under the age of 12.

With her bright and warm persona, Mathilde projects the confidence of someone with no need to win anyone over – she refuses to fill the air with chatter.   From time to time she lets silence linger, almost daring me to break it.   Because I have come seeking her story, I, of course, do.

What was the hardest part in the early days of Geneva Two?

Everything was hard. We were bursting with ideals, but our plans to embody those ideals were, at best, poorly formed.

Give me one example.

Sharing.

Here, Mathilde gives me my first taste of her capacity to linger in silence.

OK you've got to give me a bit more than that. We all learn to share as children.   To a degree that's basic Christianity, isn't it? If a man asks for your coat, give him your cloak also ... love your neighbor, that kind of thing?

Right. There's this Christian expectation that everyone shares when they have a little extra, when it's convenient and fits our schedule and budget. That's good. But we dreamed about inconvenient sharing. Sharing that pressed us to re-think our budgets and re-prioritize our calendars; sharing that pushed us to the point where it hurt. We wanted to share so deeply that people would wonder if we were sane. "Radical sharing" is what Jake called it. Kyle thought that didn't sound theological enough. After a lot of long, boring arguments, the boys finally settled on the phrase "covenanted stewards."

Language games are nice. What did this look like in day to day living?

The obvious starter for us was to have common meals. We decided to share dinner together every night, each home taking turns hosting.

That's pretty ambitious.

Yes, it was.

And how did it go?

It bombed. *Another extended silence.*

I don't suppose you could elaborate?

She laughs softly. Sure. It's hard enough to schedule time for one family to be together, much less four. Within the first month we were simmering with frustration.

Of course Nathan and Kyle were bull-headed about it. They insisted that we could make it work; they were smitten with the idea of making this grand prophetic statement about community. So we tried harder, and the harder we tried, the angrier we became. Everyone felt they were giving more than receiving. Each person felt she was compromising more than her fair share. No one thought anyone else was deferring.

So what happened?

When you get fed up enough, you do something, right? Andrea, Marissa, Rose and I got together one morning – right here at Ground Up. We admitted that what we were doing wasn't working. Then we started the hard work of letting go.

Letting go? Of the vision of community?

No. Letting go of our inept tactics for achieving the vision. Together we resolved that we would not wreck our ideal of radical sharing on the rocks of a single idea about how to share. That was a real turning point where our ideals began to move beyond mere words. Instead of talking about community, we started cultivating community among ourselves.

And what does cultivating community look like in this case?

The first go-round didn't work, right? And that caused conflict, right? So we reminded one another of the big goal of living as covenanted stewards, but more importantly we reaffirmed our commitment to one another. We took time to tell one another how valuable these relationships are.

And that helped?

It's not unlike marriage – you don't stop telling your husband how much you love him once you've exchanged vows. You confirm your love through habits. You speak loving words and do loving deeds. Community is the same way: you have to build habits that continually affirm the value of the relationships. So we took time to remind each other of the love and affection that God had grown among our families. We reminded one another that God called us together in this place and this time for this purpose of building a different kind of community.

What about the shared meals, then?

We rebooted the idea. *Yet another long silence.*

By which you mean?

We incorporated the lessons we had learned about the constraints on our lives, and we started over from scratch.

And how did that work?

Within an hour's conversation, we had negotiated a more workable schedule. The community would share meals two nights a week: Friday night and Sunday night. Friday night would be a little earlier and quicker, a kickoff to the weekend. We deliberately planned Sunday as a long, lingering meal with a bit more craftsmanship in the menu.

And that worked?

It worked great for a couple of years, until the community outgrew it. Then the structure stopped working.

Why was that?

Success. *By this point, I anticipate the long silences, and jump right in with followup questions.*

OK, isn't success a good thing? How did it cause problems?

When we started, we were cooking food for the core families and a couple of the boys from Single Brothers. We had a few people in the neighborhood, like the Chamblisses, who joined us for the dinners. Everyone pitched in. Dinners were a chaotic ballet of activity. But even with the chaos, the work was reasonably shared without a lot of stress.

Then the *Cincinnati Examiner* ran that article on our community. It was November 2004. Within days, we had a couple of dozen calls and emails from people interested in what we were doing. Of course we invited people to come and see what we were about. Pretty soon, the numbers at our meals doubled. We went from about 15 people to 30 to 40 in a matter of months.

That's a pretty big change. All of those people joined the community?

No, but some of them did. Others were sightseers, intrigued by the novelty of it all – they came and hung out with us for a few months, and then disappeared. However, we did have a few neighborhood families officially join. And over the next few years, several people who saw that article moved into the neighborhood as houses became available.

But that initial influx of people happened around the same time we were separating from Trinity church. We had stress piled upon stress. We were establishing ourselves as an independent organization, and at the same time the number of people participating grew rapidly. When you cross a threshold of a certain number of people, organization becomes exponentially more complicated.

The "chaotic ballet" had become a spectator show. Some folks came to our meals, but had no idea how to help out. Others felt like they got stuck with a disproportionate burden of food preparation and cleanup. We had so many people that it was hard to effectively prepare and serve a meal; a single home's kitchen and dining room just couldn't accommodate the crowd. Some of us in the original group started resenting the newer people. Something had to give.

So you had another meltdown?

Not quite. We saw a meltdown coming; we'd learned from our previous experience, so we decided to reboot the system and reprogram. I suggested that we divide the community into sharing groups. The organizing of it all fell to me – it was my idea, therefore my responsibility, right? I thought my idea was simple: once a month, I would plan a community-wide Sunday dinner, but the rest of the month, each group had to arrange for its own shared meals.

And how did that work out?

Another bomb. A flaming, sizzling disaster.

What went wrong?

Not enough clear leadership.

What kind of problems did that lack of leadership create?

No one knew who was supposed to be organizing in each group, so everyone kept looking at me to tell them what to do. People were really frustrated. So, we had another get together here at the coffee shop. Design, fail, evaluate, re-design. We'd done this before, so we knew we could do it again.

We identified people to organize the shared meals in the groups. We set up a rotation for hosting those meals, so no one family had too much on their plate. I still coordinate the monthly large group gathering, at least the food part of it. We decided to expand that monthly gathering to include a time of worship – singing and teaching. Kyle and Nathan coordinate the worship, I handle the meal. It's been working pretty well.

It sounds like getting there was pretty messy, though.

It was.

Why do you think it was so hard?

Sharing is easy, until you commit to sharing consistently. Most people feel good about sharing their things once or twice, but committing to a lifestyle of sharing takes work – it takes brainstorming how you go about doing things. It takes committing to sharing even when you don't feel compassionate or giving. It's irritating and annoying, but eventually you work it out.

OK. So sharing of meals has worked out after lots of trial and error. Surely there was someplace where you failed in learning how to share.

Of course.

Would you mind telling me about it?

Back in 2003, after the Klines and the Edmonds bought their houses here in the neighborhood, we all sold our cars and bought one community van to be shared by the four families.

That *is* a bit radical. Why did you do that?

It seemed logical. We were all in the same neighborhood. We could take group trips to the store, carpool to work, schedule turns to take the car out in the evening, combine trips. By all of us pooling our money into one van, each family would save on insurance, gas, taxes, and maintenance. The van is a flexible vehicle – good for hauling stuff, kids, groups. For shorter trips, we could bike or walk. It seemed to make sense to us.

What went wrong?

It was too constraining.

I can only imagine. Care to elaborate?

Well, Nathan's job alone requires him to have a vehicle to pick up supplies and deliver finished pieces of furniture to customers. He needed access to the vehicle a lot, which meant that others would not have access.

Forging a community requires a balance of deference to others and sticking up for yourself. Our little group has a disproportionate number of entrepreneurs who need transportation for business purposes. Having only one van among us ratcheted up tensions so tightly that it was threatening everything else we were working on. We needed to relieve the tension fast. So, for the greater good of the community, we gave up on that one little aspect.

So why keep trying? It seems like you court disaster and frustration every time you try an initiative in sharing.

Maybe. Yes, we get frustrated a lot, but learning is born out of frustration, right? The ideal of radical sharing pushes us to think about what we really need – and how we can use what we have to contribute to others. The frustration pushes us to find

25

new ways to radically share in a fundamentally individualistic society. I've come to think that community, in part, is a matter of giving one another permission to be frustrating.

So you worked out a different arrangement with the vehicles.

Sure. Once the tension was over, we saw that we could share vehicles in a responsible way.

And how did that work out?

Kyle and Marissa bought a truck. They make that truck available to anyone in the community who has a need for hauling stuff. Jake and Andrea, on the other hand, bought a small fuel-efficient sedan that is really efficient for long trips. Nathan and I have a large family, so we bought out everyone else's share in the van. We're the ones who got the most use out of it, anyway.

It was like the community got a little fleet of cars. Now, when there's a particular need, we just trade keys. That way, everyone has access to transportation when they need it.

But what if there's an accident?

Hasn't happened yet.

That doesn't mean it won't. You have to consider that possibility. Isn't it risky to keep trading vehicles like that?

Of course it's risky. Life is risky. You took a risk walking out of the door this morning. If you spend your life avoiding risk, you'll never live. God says to let the day's worries be sufficient for the day – you know that verse: consider the lilies of the field, they neither toil nor spin, but even Solomon wasn't clothed as beautifully. How much more value are you than they?

Right, but Jesus doesn't mean that we should engage in irresponsibility. There's another verse about counting the costs.

Well sure. Jesus didn't preach irresponsibility. He did, however, say not to worry. We all carry insurance, we all are licensed drivers by the state of Ohio, we all have made promises to one another that we're covenanted stewards – we're in the business of wise use of our shared resources. We've reasonably faced the risks, so why worry, right?

We're here because we are called by God to be here. No one goes through the trouble and inconvenience of joining this community unless they experience God's calling, unless they feel it in their gut like a magnet pulling them forward. It's that sense of calling that gives us a foundation of trust in one another. Every time we have trouble and pain in working issues out, we later discover that the difficulties were God tools for shaping us, for leading us to trust one another more deeply.

Even if there is a car accident or if something goes wrong, I don't think we'll look at it as a disaster. We'll face it as a family of faith. It's not irresponsible to trust one another, but it is impoverishing to go through life never taking the risk of living in a relationship of trust.

Our conversation turns to triathalons, training, and sports nutrition. Mathilde encourages me in my hopes of one day running a marathon. She promises to send me an email link to a marathon training program that she followed for the Chicago Marathon.

The Geneva Two Compact
July 2002

We, the undersigned, compact ourselves to a Christian covenanted community. As such a covenant community, we hold the following principles.

1. We are **Romantic Realists**. The world is broken and marred. Unlike idealists who believe in human perfection, we admit this brokenness. However, God has not left this broken world to its own devices. Unlike the cynics who see this world as going to hell in a handbasket, we see the purposefulness and beauty that God has worked into creation.

2. We are **Covenanted Stewards**. We recognize that we are given individual responsibilities, and that we are also made for society. Our possessions are our own, but they are given to us that we may bless others. Unlike Communists, we believe private property is essential to good stewardship. Unlike Darwinists, we believe that we have a responsibility to each other, and thus we are not engaged in a pitted battle of "survival of the fittest."

3. We are **Culture Creators**. God has given us the cultural mandate to build Godly culture. Jesus sends his people to be salt and light in the world. We believe that Christians are to pursue truth, goodness, and beauty in the public squares of the world. In such pursuit, God will be glorified. Unlike isolationists, we do not pull away from culture to huddle in our own enclave. Unlike accomodationists, we believe that God has called us to exert dominion over culture, rather than be influenced by it.

Guided by these principles, we make the following commitments to one another:

1. We will live in physical proximity to one another, defined as being within a 10-15 minute walk of one another, ideally living in the same neighborhood.
2. We will generously share our resources with one another, preferring lending and borrowing to getting and spending.
3. We will encourage one another in simplicity, creating a balancing voice against the consumerism rampant in our culture.
4. We will show the beauty of the Lord by encouraging one another in creativity, striving to actively create rather than passively consume.
5. We will seek to transform the larger community by exerting God's dominion over all spheres of human endeavor: arts, politics, education, business, and social organization.
6. We will meet weekly as a community group to encourage one another to grow in holiness through admonition.
7. We will regularly and generously give of our financial resources to bless the frail, the marginalized, and the needy.
8. We will submit to the authority and leadership of the teaching and ruling elders of Trinity Presbyterian Church.

Kyle Edmonds

Kyle Edmonds meets me out front of his Oneida Street home. The slight stoop in his broad, rounded, shoulders hides his true stature. He is not overweight, yet by any account he is a large man: thick in the arms, the neck, the shoulders, his chest. The breeze plays with his shaggy brown hair, but he does not notice, for his attention is fully fixed on greeting me. His eyes reflect a mélange of sadness and merriment.

As we talk, Kyle walks me through his elaborate and expansive back garden, which he has designed as an alternative to the traditional lawn. Kyle trains my eye to see that the intricate interplay of plants is not only a decorative arrangement, but also a productive vegetable garden. Hostas give shade to baby lettuces; scarlet runner beans cover the fence. I cannot begin to adequately explain how this garden combines azaleas, tomatoes, broccoli and astilbe. Ajuga competes with a compact watermelon vine for groundcover space. Peas and beans and carrots peek from beneath manicured boxwoods.

As we walk the paths through this densely packed landscape, Kyle seasons our conversation with not-so-brief asides about compost, plant arrangement, microclimates, nitrogen fixers, and permaculture. He occasionally bends to pluck a weed. From time to time, he stops our conversation, pulling aside a branch to show a feature or explain the unique properties of a hidden plant. For the reader's sanity, I have edited out these horticultural asides.

First, let me thank you again for persuading the community to allow me do these interviews.

My pleasure. I must admit it was an uphill battle. Your reputation precedes you. Your articles on religion tend to put people of faith in a less than flattering light.

Yes, I've been told I have a bit of an acid pen. Hazard of the trade, I suppose.

I must warn you that some of our people are still worried about talking with you. They're afraid you might steamroll right over them.

I doubt anyone could steamroll over Mrs. Van Doehrn.
Point well taken.

What about you? Are you afraid of the big bad secular journalist?

Kyle offers a wry grin. He answers in a tone that is serious but not threatened. It is a solemn kindness, a weightiness without stuffiness. I trust you. Your work has been about puncturing the inflated egos of the Christian celebrity culture. We're on the fringe. We're not asking for hagiography, just fairness. I believe that you will be fair.

Well, I'll do my best to honor your confidence. So let's start at the beginning. How did you and Marissa become involved in Geneva Two?

It grew out of a small group study at Trinity Presbyterian. Nathan and Mathilde Probisco, the Hoffeckers, the Klines, the Smiths, and Marissa and myself. The whole church was studying the Biblical concepts of community. Pastor Poteat asked each member to participate in a small group study in which they would read and reflect upon Bonhoeffer's *Life Together*.

That book kicked our collective tuckuses. For my part, I felt spiritually flabby and weak in the light of Bonhoeffer's robust vision of Christian community. We all did. That's the value, I suppose, of reading classic books; the saints of the past reveal our present weaknesses with a clarity that many contemporary commentators lack.

Anyway, our group decided to stay together and study the topic of community more deeply. We spent a year or so meeting each week and picking apart different biblical passages about community, about care for one another, and about the calling to be Christ's body.

That sounds a bit excessive, don't you think? Most small group studies are, as I recall, just a few weeks long.

We found it refreshing. Remember, this was the late 90s – it was a time saturated in irony and isolation. People were changing jobs and moving cross-country to chase ever-escalating salaries. To get ahead, you had to stand out with attitude and flash. To be young and active meant to be jaded, cynical, and self-absorbed.

Not much has changed since then, has it?

Kyle chuckles kindly. Perhaps not. But seriously, is that how we're supposed to live? After a steady diet of narcissism, the soul hungers for more healthful fare, doesn't it? We're made for community; it nourishes us and helps us to thrive. Of course we can survive in isolation, but God designed us in such a way that we flourish in relationships – relationships of trust and mutual giving to one another. It's at the root of what it means to be human.

So after that year of study, Nathan proposed we start thinking about something more concrete. He and Jake had been talking about what it would look like if we all agreed to live close to one another – to share with one another. We started reading up on ideas like New Monasticism, intentional community, and cohousing.

By then, things started moving pretty fast. We all went away for a weekend of fasting and prayer in January of 2002. Four of the five couples felt God leading us to a deeper form of intentional community. The Smiths were the only ones who didn't feel led that way. That was a hard decision for all of us – we all knew that those families who were in would experience a new level of closeness that would radically change the nature of the relationships.

Jake took on the job of drafting our community agreement – what would eventually become the Geneva Compact. Meanwhile, I led us in weekly prayer sessions as we sought God's direction on how this would turn out. The Probiscos and the

Klines took the lead on scouting out neighborhoods that had available housing stock for four families. By June of that year we finalized the first version of the compact and identified this neighborhood as the place we wanted to move.

It took us a year or so, but we all finally moved into the neighborhood by June 2003. By that time Alan Gasque had joined us and started the Single Brothers House. It was an exciting time. We were building a new community right in the middle of the neighborhood – a community based on deep relationships – a community rooted in all the "one another" statements that Jesus offers up in the New Testament. Our goal was to show the goodness of Christ through the quality of the relationships among His people.

A noble ideal. But can't relationships go bad? Co-dependent people are in relationships. Passive aggression and abuse all have to exist in a relationship with someone.

Fair enough. We human beings are very good at making an unsavory hash out of our relationships. Left to our own devices, we consume one another like tasty morsels from a buffet. We are weak and selfish at heart. But remember that we also understand that we are in deep need of God's grace for any of our relationships to survive.

So God gives you the strength to not consume one another?

Yes, though I'll go a step further. God, in His very character, gives us the design for relationships.

OK, I'm afraid you're losing me. Can you unpack that a bit, please?

Sure – let's sit for a moment. *He motions to a pair of wooden Adirondack chairs, positioned beneath a cluster of dwarf apple trees in the back corner of the lot. We have travelled to the heart of the garden and are surrounded by color and liveliness.* God has revealed himself as a

Trinity. Three persons: Father, Son, and Holy Spirit; one being. Not three *ideas,* or three *concepts,* or three *facets.* We're not talking about three *roles* of the being of God. Nor do we mean three *senses* in which we understand God's character.

We understand the Trinity as three persons who *are persons* – with personality, aims, talents, aspirations, and capacity to love and be loved. Yet they are three persons in *one* being. It's a mysterious and baffling concept, because we're not talking about three separate gods. The three persons are distinctive enough to be considered unique, but so united in power and love and being that they can only be thought of as one entity.

Lots of people have problems with the Trinity.

The only way I can get my brain around the Trinity is to understand that relationship – defined as healthy, committed giving and receiving of love – is a fundamental aspect of God's character. And therefore, the one God exists as three persons.

Some theologians talk about the "attributes" of God: power, justice, holiness, wisdom, eternality, etc. You're saying that "relationship" is one of them?

It's what sets the Christian understanding apart. In other faiths, they understand the gods as being *in* relationship – with one another, with humans, with creation. Those relationships are fraught with the strife, tension, and conflict that make mythology so interesting.

However, the doctrine of the Trinity is different. God, as a single being certainly has relationships with everything else in creation. But God, existing from eternity as a Triune community, *defines* what it is to be in relationship. God *is* relationship.

And therefore relationship is God?

Again, a chuckle, not of condescension, but of genuine mirth. That would be a tempting corollary, wouldn't it? But, no, that is not the case. A subset does not equal the whole set. All cows eat grass, but not all grass-eaters are cows.

Let's make the analogy with beauty. Beauty is an aspect of God – God, being God, gets to define beauty. And as creator, God has woven beauty all throughout creation.

Suppose we find a hint of beauty in the midst of ugliness: a wildflower growing in a pile of refuse, for instance. We have not suddenly creatively re-defined beauty. Rather, our finite and limited minds have glimpsed a bit of grace. We grasp that God, even in the darkest places, has not abandoned His creation. The question that ought to arise in our minds is: "if this is beautiful, even in the midst of decay and destruction, how much more beautiful might it be in a redeemed world?"

And you suggest the same is true for relationships?

Did you ever read *Les Miserables*?

I saw the musical.

Good choice, but the book is better. We're bookish people here in Geneva Two – one of the hazards of intentional community, I suppose. *He chuckles, as though this were meant to be humorous.*

When you read the book, you'll find that it's Victor Hugo's extended parable about Christian life in troubled times. He writes this wonderful scene in which the impoverished and desperate single mother, Fantine, is searching for someone to care for her daughter. Passing by a country inn, she sees a woman, the innkeeper Madame Thernardier, in a moment of domestic tenderness with her children. Fantine is so impressed by the warmth she observes, that she begs Madame Thernardier to take her daughter. She has no way of knowing that the Thernardiers are greedy monsters who will cruelly exploit her daughter. She sees only the moment of kindness, not the darkness of their hearts.

I'm not sure I get where you're going ...

Simply this: the great villains all have mundane moments of domestic tranquility. In *The Merchant of Venice*, Shylock's greatest moment is his one line mourning the loss of a ring given him by his deceased wife Judith. We certainly don't equate these villains with godliness – but their very human-ness invites us to ask, "What wonders might we see if this villain were renewed and redeemed by God?"

Let's back up for a moment. You've taken an imaginative jump from God's relationships within the Trinity to human relationships with one another. That's a bit of a logical flaw, don't you think?

Not so much. Scripture teaches that every human, every man woman and child, is made as a bearer of the *image* of God. The longer I live, the grander and more breathtaking I find that truth. It gives foundation to so many lesser truths that we hold dear: the dignity of human life; the inner creative drive of the human spirit; the fundamental equality of all people; the foundational rights of life, liberty, and the pursuit of happiness. So much of all that is transcendent and life affirming finds its origins in the bedrock truth of humanity being made in the image of God.

And that is true of our relationships as well. We yearn for love and connection and sharing because we were *made* for it. We were *made* to enjoy community with one another and with God. Remember, God as Trinity has both one-to-one relationships and one-to-many. The Father has a relationship with the Son and a relationship with the Spirit, but the Father also has a relationship to the whole community consisting of Son *and* Spirit *and* himself. We're the same. I have a relationship with each individual in the Geneva Two community, but I also have a relationship with the community as a whole.

When we dream of how relationships *ought* to be, we're dreaming for a bit of the inter-Trinitarian life. When we're at our most generous, our most outgoing, our most kind and loving, we're aspiring to honor the image of God in one another. We long for relationship in which we are absolutely sure and secure in our identity – comfortable in our own skins as it were. Yet at the same time, we want to be in relationships in which we are deeply connected with and giving to the other. This godly kind of relationship both honors the dignity of the other while not negating the dignity of the self. Our human relationships can only aspire to the true relationship enjoyed by God.

OK, we have gotten into deep waters really quickly. We all aspire to the quality of the Trinitarian relationships. Jesus calls us into relationship with him and one another. Interesting ideas. How do these ideas help with practical living in your daily relationships?

Answer me this: can you truly be in relationship with someone and remain unchanged?

Could you possibly tell your wife or your beloved or your dear friend that you have been untouched and unmoved by being in relationship with them? Would you dare to say, "I love you, my dear, but I am completely unmoved to be different from what I was before we met"? We don't call that love – we call that indifference. We call that treating someone as a convenience or as window dressing. If a man did that to a woman, we'd call him a cad. If a father did that to a child we'd call him aloof and cold. Why then would we expect to be in relationship with God and be unchanged?

What's more, why would we expect to be placed into a community of people who are all in relationship with Christ and be unchanged? And why would we not expect people in the community to be in the process of being changed? Even more, what leads us to believe that that process of change and growth stops in this lifetime?

I've heard this kind of rhetoric in Christian circles before. The application of practical principles requires some kind of mystical encounter with Jesus. This is the 'that's why you need Jesus, too' part, right? The part where you ask me to 'ask Jesus into my heart'?

Kyle leans forward in his chair and fixes me with a serious gaze. He takes on a more solemn tone than I have heard from him thus far. You can't understand our community without understanding the Jesus part. Neither can you understand any true Christian community without understanding the Jesus part. Most importantly, you can't understand Christian community without grasping that Jesus isn't merely an idea or a much-admired teacher, but the living king who calls individuals into relationship with Him. And when we are in relationship with Him, he calls us into particular relationships with the rest of His people. Just like the Trinity – one-to-one relationships and one-to-many relationships.

OK, let's grant all that for a moment...

Kyle stands up, and I rise along with him. He drops his serious tone. He is firm, but there is no heat – rather, he's almost playful, as though he were inviting me in on a secret. Hathcer, I'm afraid I didn't put it up for debate. It is not even an *a priori* intellectual concept. Among us, relationship with Jesus is an experienced reality. You will understand neither our community nor our way of being until you grasp that truth. You can accept the validity of our experience or not – your choice.

He claps me on the shoulder and smiles broadly. C'mon, let's have some lunch.

We wind our way back through the garden, exchanging more talk about plants and gardening. When we arrive in the house, we see that Marissa has laid out a lunch of fresh salad, BLT sandwiches, and homemade potato chips. The Edmonds' three children are waiting patiently. Kyle offers a prayer before the meal – it is a longer prayer than I am used to, earnest and heartfelt rather than perfunctory.

After eating, I help Kyle clear the dishes while Marissa starts packing to take the children for an afternoon trip to the zoo.

Let me follow up on something. If 'the Jesus part' is the most critical part of understanding the Geneva Two community, then what would you say is the clearest sign of Jesus in your midst?

Worship.

That's it? Simply going to church?

Aha! That's it and that's not it. Worship is so very much more than "going to church."

What is it then?

Worship is the meeting of divine and human relationships. Worship is our living our whole lives to glorify God and to enjoy Him. But more narrowly, when we talk about a gathering of God's people to glorify Him, that is worship. As we gather and hear God's Word, we trust that His Spirit works on us. We trust that the Spirit applies the word to our hearts and leads us into greater depth of relationship.

Oh come on. That's still going to church.

As much as going to the theater makes you an actor or going to a concert makes you a musician. We might attend a worship service at a large church – we might go with the attitude of a consumer of religious goods and services, evaluating the cost and benefit – as though the pastor were little more than a shopkeeper competing for our business. I don't doubt that God works in those situations and nudges our hearts and quietly shapes us. But that's not what we mean by worship.

What we mean is our deliberate gathering around God's word. We mean our expectation that Christ will work on us. We mean our realization that Christ has bound us together. Worship becomes the place where we enjoy with a little more clarity the inter-Trinitarian love, and it is the venue in which, by the attentive work of the Holy Spirit, we are sharpened to live out that love.

Worship is part of the fabric of our community – we begin and close the day with prayers in our homes. We meet with one another and pray for one another all through the week. Each week, we enjoy more formal liturgical worship in small-group gatherings throughout the community. Once a month we gather the entire community for an exuberant celebratory worship. Worship is a lived reality because Jesus is a living reality among us.

So that's why you withdrew into a community – so you could experience this "living reality" of Jesus?

No. That experience should happen in any church, large or small, high or low. We should all expect to experience the reality of Jesus Christ in our lives. That is what it is to be Christian.

Long before we dreamed about Geneva Two, we had experienced the reality of Jesus in our lives. This community exists simply in obedience to Jesus' particular calling on *our* lives. That's why you have to understand the Jesus part. The call of Jesus is different for each of His disciples. Yes, there is a general sense in which all Christians are called to be disciples. But beyond that there is a *particular* calling for each Christian. Over time, Jesus molds our lives around that calling. Everyone here has experienced a particular calling to live in this community. We know it's not for everyone, but it is for us. Jesus confirms that calling in our hearts by making us feel an ever-deepening commitment to one another and to the community that we're building here.

As we finish the dishes, Kyle turns the conversation toward my work as a reporter. We talk for another fifteen minutes or so, until Mathilde Probisco pulls up out front with her van. Marissa and Mathilde exchange keys – the Probiscos are loaning the Edmonds their van for the afternoon. Marissa bundles the three children into the van while Kyle and I say our goodbyes. Mathilde walks up the street back to her house, while I take my final notes and savor the aroma of lavender that wafts from the front garden.

Mike Schulman

I'm treating Mike Schulman to lunch at Ridge View Chili. When the nation takes note of the culinary scene in and around Cincinnati, it speaks first of the region's two chains of chili parlors: Overlook Chili and Bullseye Chili. What is less known, however, are the independent neighborhood chili parlors, each defying the homogeneity of the chains. Ridge View Chili sports a retro-50's décor, complete with jukebox, vintage photos, laminate counters, teal vinyl seats, and a vintage pastry case laden with cheesecake and pies. Our waitress wears a clean white apron and calls me "Hon." The smell of grease hangs in the air, seeping into my clothes, my skin, my hair.

Mike is a Gulf War veteran. When we first met at the picnic, I saw in his face an all too familiar mask-like quality – not a mask of deception, but rather of compassion, like the way parents shield their children from "adult themes" when they talk. At the picnic, we talked very little about the war. Instead, he told me about his present work at Geneva Farms, an organic heirloom-vegetable farm founded by Maria Sanchez, another former member of the Geneva Two community. He is working with a group to plant a Geneva Two offshoot community around the farm.

At this meeting at Ridge View Chili, we spend most of the meal talking about his childhood, his work on the farm, and Jazz. It is only when our plates are cleared and we have ordered coffee and banana cream pie that we are relaxed enough to talk about how he came to Geneva Two.

Tell me about coming home from the service.

Mike sighs. I served two tours in Iraq. Ur of the Chaldees, Chaplain Fary called it. *He shrugs and offers a faint smile.* Dad didn't like that I'd enlisted. I never understood what the difficulty was, but there it is. So, I got out of the army, and I wasn't about to go crying to him for help. Problem was, I didn't know what to do with civilian life.

"Didn't know what to do...." Tell me more about that.

The Army is all about structure and focus. Each soldier has a clear job and a defined place. You don't stop being you … you just know that you're a part of something bigger. And there are people who count on you, and you count on them. If you don't do what you're supposed to do, people die. You might die even if everyone *is* doing what they're supposed to do.

The point is, you have a place. Everyone has a place. Even though you might die, you have some security in knowing your place. It's something you can plant your feet on.

But after two tours, I was done. I wanted to keep going, but I couldn't. All my reserves were spent. I felt hollowed out, like a Halloween pumpkin. So, I didn't re-enlist. I came home.

I had no idea that I would miss it so much.

Miss it. You mean the Army?

The structure. The community. The mission. While I was in the sandbox, we had a clear mission. We trusted each other. We counted on each other. We had respect for one another, you know? It was intense. We had this job that we came to do, and we worked hard. All of us wanted to get the job done and get back home.

When I did get back, that was all gone. No community, no purpose. I was on my own.

Adrift and on your own. Had you thought about what you were going to do after the service?

No. I didn't have a clue.

Did you get any help – from the government or from churches?

I didn't think to ask. I figured I was a competent and capable guy. I followed orders well. How hard could it be to hold a regular job?

I tried a sales job for a while, but the boss was dishonest – wanted me to outright lie to clients so that we could clinch the sale. It made me sick – that's not the kind of life I had signed up to defend. So I quit. I bounced around to a couple of different things, but always felt restless.

Then I took this job with a paint crew. It paid the bills. It paid for liquor. Looking back, I was just numbing myself. A lot of times, painting is solo work. It can be really peaceful – put the earbuds in and zone out to John Coltrane's *A Love Supreme*. And when you're not working, a fifth of cheap bourbon helps to keep you numb. Pretty soon, I was showing up to work drunk, trying to hide that fact. It didn't matter much; most of the rest of the crew were stoners anyway. I just spiraled down. Better to feel nothing than face the pain, you know?

Sounds like it was rough.

I hit bottom. I went on a binge - missed work for a week. That got me fired. Pretty soon I was on the streets living in a shelter downtown. Sounds like a cliché, doesn't it – vet comes home, and his life falls apart?

It's your story. No one's story is cliché.

I know lots of guys who came back and adjusted fine. I saw an article in the paper the other week about some vets in Baltimore who decided to use their training to work on a blighted neighborhood, bringing it back to life. We did a lot of community building in Iraq, you know? It wasn't just fighting all the time – we tried to help build, too. But nobody ever tells that story about the army – it's just roadside bombs and firefights in the papers.

Anyway, these guys figured out how to re-deploy their urban operations and humanitarian aid skills. They brought the mission home, in a way. Or maybe they filled the void with a new mission. I wish I could've figured that out sooner rather than later.

Anyway, there I was down at the shelter. Dad found out. He came down and yanked me out of there and paid for rehab at one of those high-end recovery places, you know? Dad said that he wasn't going to let me go to 'some homeless mission in an inner city war zone.' *Laughs.* Funny, right? As though urban poverty was more dangerous that what I'd already been through … he just had no clue.

So how did you get from there to Geneva Two?

So, every so often during rehab, I'd check in with Chaplain Fary via email. He was with our unit during our second tour, and I trusted him like no one else. He was different. He could drink with the rest of us, cuss like the rest of us, and he had no problem riding with us in dangerous zones. In fact he seemed to seek out danger. He said that we were his flock, and our dangers were his dangers. I felt like he got it, you know? So when I needed help, I checked in with him.

He got you plugged in at Geneva Two?

Not directly. I was living in this halfway house, the last stage of the rehab program. One day I get this call from a Reverend Poteat. He tells me that Chaplain Fary and he are old friends and that the Chaplain had asked him to pay me a visit. Rev. Poteat had moved out of town, but he was back for a visit. He asked if he could introduce me to some of his friends who might be able to help me after I graduated from the program. I said sure.

So Rev. Poteat came by, picked me up. We drove over to Ground Up, and he introduced me to Nathan Probisco and Alan Gasque. Alan was starting this thing with renting out rooms to men. One thing led to another, and I signed up.

So it was simply a rental arrangement then? You weren't signing up to be a part of the community?

Not at first. I just needed someplace stable, you know? I needed a place of my own. I couldn't go back to mom and dad's

– too much stress, too much guilt. But anyplace I could afford would be in a really bad neighborhood. I wasn't afraid of crime or violence, but I really didn't need to be around the scene in those neighborhoods.

Alan was doing something different. He had a four-bedroom house and his goal was to rent out three of the rooms to young men.

But what was so different about Alan's rental agreement?

So, Alan's idea was that we had to agree to certain rules – including rules about chores and cleaning the house. He was really disciplined about identifying whose food was whose – everything in the cabinets was labeled with someone's name.

Alan took time to figure out who was good at what and tried to divide the work evenly and fairly. Oh yeah, there was no alcohol, either. That was a draw for me. We had one or two other guys that came for a while, but they couldn't handle the policy, so they left. Alan's point wasn't that alcohol was bad. He was trying to make sure the house wasn't a party house.

Wasn't it difficult to live in a house with so many people?

I wouldn't have thought so. I was in the Army. I was used to living together with a bunch of guys. But this was different. It was more structured than most roommate situations, but lots less structured than the Army. To tell the truth, some of these cats didn't take well to any structure at all.

I had a few shouting matches, like when someone didn't take his turn cleaning up or mowing the yard. I'm usually pretty laid back, but I had this bad tendency to hold stuff in until I snapped. And boy, would I snap hard. Rehab helped a lot with that, but this living arrangement really tested me.

That's where Alan helped. He'd pull me aside and very calmly coach me through how to confront people without lashing out at them.

Can you tell me about one of those confrontations?

So, there was this guy named Park. He was this frat-boy type right out of college. He had some kind of high-pressure sales job. Looking back, I think he only took the room at Alan's as a stopgap until he could arrange something better.

Park was the laziest guy I'd ever seen, at least when it came to helping out. Maybe he worked hard at his job, but he sure didn't get the idea of group responsibility for the house. His pop cans and nacho cheese chip bags littered the living room. He only took his turn vacuuming and dusting if one of us rode his back until it was done, but that was difficult because he hardly spent any time at the house. He'd come back from work, get changed, and go right back out again, not stumbling back until 3 in the morning. Then he'd be up at 6:30 the next day, getting showered and ready to go into work. He had to be doing some massive amphetamines to be able to sustain that pace.

Anyway, I wake up late one night – a bad dream. I go out to the kitchen to get some water when I find Park in there. He must've just gotten in a late night at the clubs; he was pretty drunk. Well, he has my jar of peanut butter – we label the food, remember? There's no way he couldn't know it was mine. So, he's got my jar of peanut butter and he's dipping his fingers into it and sucking the peanut butter off his fingers. Then he dips his wet fingers back into the jar for another scoop.

I say, 'Hey! That's my peanut butter!'

And Park looks at me with this look of contempt -- I think that's what set me off – no respect, you know. He doesn't say sorry. He doesn't even pretend to be clueless. He looks at me as though he was well within his rights and I was the one being petty bringing this up.

Then like a sassy five year old, he says 'I thought we were all supposed to *share*.'

He pauses for a moment. The tip of his finger traces along the rim of the coffee cup in front of him. When he speaks again, his voice is pitched a fine shade higher.

Park had pushed me one too many times. So I grabbed the front of his shirt and threw him out of the kitchen into the dining room. He crashed into the table and started cussing up a storm. He tried to turn around, but I was on him in a blind rage. I think I was trying to turn him around and pin his arms behind his back, just so I could teach him a lesson. And he hollered and clawed at my face. So I punched him in the gut. Two or three times. We wrestled like that for a few moments, and then the other guys in the house were pulling us off each other. Everyone was shouting and then Alan was standing there between the two of us.

'Both of you get to your rooms,' Alan said. 'We'll talk about this in the morning.' Alan didn't yell or shout. He wasn't overly stern or anything. He was calm and quiet, but I knew that he meant what he said. The terms of our rental agreement were clear: violence was grounds for immediate eviction. I knew he was going to kick me out. This community was good for me, but I'd blown my chance. I nodded and went to my room.

As I was going, I heard Park do the stupidest thing he could do – he protested. 'He attacked me! He jumped all over me just because I was eating his peanut butter! I want him gone!'

'Park,' Alan said calmly yet firmly, 'go to bed, sober up.'

'Oh come on! He started it. Why are you yelling at me?'

Alan kept his calm, 'Park, I'm telling you for the last time. Go to bed. You are on very thin ice right now….'

'I'M on thin ice? I'm the one who's been attacked and somehow I'm on thin ice?'

'ENOUGH. It's like I'm talking with a three year old. You come in every night drunk to the gills. You're rude, disrespectful, and you don't pull your weight in chores. I've tried to graciously talk with you about these things and you keep blowing them off. You've shown yourself to be spoiled, self-centered, and a royal pain! Now get to bed and plan on calling in late to work tomorrow because you and I are going to talk about your future here.'

I heard Park slam the door to his room. I didn't sleep a bit that night.

Next day, Alan told me that we'd speak at lunchtime. I went in to work as usual. I came back for lunch, and Alan met me.

'Alan, I'm sorry,' I said, 'I lost control. He was driving me up the wall. I know there's no excuse for it. I should control myself better. I know that this means I've got to go. Can you just give me a couple of days, a week at most, to find something else? I promise I'll stay out of everyone's way. I'll especially avoid Park. I guess I need to apologize to him, though....'

'Park's gone,' Alan said. I was floored and didn't know what to say, so I let him continue. 'Park is a snotty, selfish, undisciplined jerk who thinks the world owes him. I see a lot of his type, but he is by far the worst. I've tried hard to correct him, but he was having none of it. He's gone.

'You lost control last night. But you know you did wrong. You've been through hell and back again. From what I've seen you understand grace because you've experienced it. This is the place for you.'

Mike stops his story. He is still and silent amidst the ambient sounds of gentle conversation, forks on plates, and kitchen noise. I wait patiently.

I felt like I had a home, the first one I'd had since the Army, you know? That week, I asked Alan if I could come to the Geneva Two worship. I went with him and he introduced me around. Kyle was teaching, and it was unlike anything I'd expected.

What was different?

He wasn't on a pedestal. He taught by asking us questions. It was kind of uncomfortable because he didn't ask easy questions that were about the content of the Bible. He asked the hard questions about how we live and how we apply the Bible to our lives. He was serious, too. Not any jokes or nice stories or poems. I guess the best way to say it is that worship didn't feel like a production or a show.

So what did it feel like, if you had to describe it?

It felt like everyone was there for a reason. They came to do something. I didn't get it at first – but they were there to work. Their work was to sing, to thank God, and to examine themselves so they could do God's work. I guess the closest analogy would be that it felt a little bit like Basic Training, only ... gentler, maybe? ... Well, not as rough on the body anyway.

It was finding a group with a mission again?

Mike is silent once more.

In rehab, they talked about surrender to a higher power. That was all good. I had this vague idea of the Force or some old English actor high on a cloud. Alan and the rest of the community put flesh on that higher power for me. They taught me to see Jesus in the life of their community.

So yeah, it was like finding a group with a mission. These were people who understood respect, they understood that they all had roles and parts to play. And it wasn't easy all the time – it hurt like hell sometimes to have to examine myself and my own motives. But it was good too.

I even found a mission that will take the rest of my life. I always thought that church was about *not* doing stuff, you know. Don't drink. Don't steal. Don't do bad things. But this idea of being Culture Creators, building Godly culture – that's a mission that excites me.

How do you know what to build? You don't have a commanding officer directing you.

But we do. The people in Geneva Two know what it is to listen to God. No one is forced by any church elder to do any mission. We're all taught to pray. We learn to listen to God.

But how do you know? How did you know that God wanted you to be a part of the Geneva Farm offshoot?

For me, it was learning to trust the inner compass. It was the same feeling that I felt when joining the Army – I just had to do it and I knew it was right. I'm learning how to trust that intuition. Kyle talks about how the Holy Spirit sanctifies our intuition over time – as we grow in prayer and our knowledge of God's word. I guess I've learned how to listen to that inner nudge.

So when Maria brought her idea for Geneva Farms to the community for prayer, I felt that inner nudge. I liked the idea of being on the ground floor of a new Geneva community. I felt drawn to the land and to the idea of farming. I guess a part of me hopes I can help shape this new community to be a safe place where recovering addicts can get out of the inner city for a while – a place where people can learn some new skills. It's a mission, and it fits.

Gary and Lynn Chamblis

Gary and Lynn Chamblis are in their early 60s. Their house on the corner of Onieda Street and New Economy Lane is easily the largest in the neighborhood. As I settle into a plush chair in their living room, I notice that every wall is lined with floor-to-ceiling bookshelves, each of them stuffed. Lynn brings us hazelnut coffee and gingersnap cookies, then nestles next to her husband on the long couch.

Gary and Lynn run the Geneva Two resource center. From noon to 8pm, anyone in the community can come into their home and avail themselves of the vast library of books, DVDs, and music CDs. Gary also keeps his garage workshop open for community members to use for free. On any given day, there might be community members coming to learn from the gardening resources, children doing homework, or people gathering to share a cup of coffee in the kitchen.

Though they have lived in the neighborhood for over 30 years, the Chamblises are not founding members of the Geneva Two community. They officially joined the community six years ago, and in the intervening time they have found their niche. Cheerful and exuberant, Lynn and Gary start talking before I get the first question out.

Lynn: I'm so glad that someone is finally doing a story on this place. We really think we've got something special here.

Gary: Lynn, we've already had a story – it ran five years ago!

Lynn: I know, but this is different. That was a story that ran in the local paper.

Gary: It was picked up by the AP and run across the country.

Lynn: It was different!

Before we go too far down that path, let's talk about your involvement with Geneva Two. You lived here long before the Geneva Two community started.

Lynn: Oh yes! We had been here for a little over 20 years when they first started. We've seen people come and go, so we didn't think much of it when a few new families moved in.

Gary: We thought they were a commune!

Lynn: Gary, stop it.

Gary: They sounded like a bunch of warmed over hippies from the '60s! I knew that first came the 'radical sharing' and next the drugs and wife swapping and free love. And then 'Hello, Marxism!'

That's a pretty harsh assessment, considering that you now are sharing your resources in a pretty radical way. What changed your mind?

Gary leans forward, fixing his eyes upon mine. Private Property. The community doesn't hold anything in common – each person is responsible for caring for their own private property. The ideal of sharing is voluntary, not strong-armed upon us by some central authority.

Weren't the communes of the '60s voluntary?

Gary: They were Marxists!

Lynn: Gary, it's an honest question. Yes, the communes were voluntary, but their ideals were completely different from ours. Those old style communes had the idea that everything was held in common and the community as a whole would agree on the right distribution. In practice, the community leaders would decide where everything went.

Gary: What my wife is politely trying to say is that whoever talked the fastest or cozied up to the deciders wound up getting all the goodies. It's the old 80/20 principle: 80 percent of the work is done by 20 percent of the people. It's *Animal Farm* in real life: the clever pigs figure out how to game the system to work everyone else to death. The horse keeps saying 'I will work harder' and in the end he gets sent to the glue factory! *Lynn gets up and searches for a book in the shelves.*

But didn't Geneva Two start with that kind of communal ownership? Mathilde told me about their car experiment.

Gary: Exactly! That's what made me suspicious of them from the get-go. You'll notice that little experiment wasn't exactly a stunning success.

Lynn pulls a book off the shelf and breaks in: The Plymouth colony went through this. They tried holding all things in common, and discovered that under that system, people didn't have the drive to work. Then in 1623, Governor Bradford assigned everyone their own plot and told them to grow their own crops. They doubled or tripled their harvest. Listen to this from *Plymouth Plantation:*

> "The failure of this experiment of communal service, which was tried for several years, and by good and honest men proves the emptiness of the theory of Plato and other ancients, applauded by some of later times − that the taking away of private property, and the possession of it in community, by a commonwealth, would make a state happy and flourishing; as if they were wiser than God. For in this instance, community of property (so far as it went), was found to breed much confusion and discontent, and retard much employment which would have been to the general benefit and comfort. For the young men who were most able and fit for service objected to being forced to spend their time and strength in working for other men's wives and children, without any recompence. The strong man or the resourceful man had no more share of food, clothes, etc. than the weak

man who was not able to do a quarter the other could. This was thought injustice."

Gary: You see? The Pilgrims learned from their mistakes. So did the first crop of Geneva Two folks. They tried it, and it failed, and so they re-structured along the lines of individual responsibility.

Then how does this idea of individual responsibility relate to what you do as part of the community? You open your home for eight hours a day. You lend out your books, your music, and your tools. I may be mistaken here, but it sure feels like you're living a communal existence.

Gary: Aha! But this was a *choice*. Nobody in the community asked us to do this. This was *our* idea – our baby. We've been blessed with a house larger than we can handle. We also happen to love books.

Lynn: And we love *talking* about books and *sharing* books. This whole thing started because we love to share, so Gary had this idea ...

Gary: It wasn't my idea, I read about it in *NewsReport* magazine.

Lynn: Anyway, Gary had this idea to build a Little Free Library. Did you see it out front as you came in?

I'm not sure...

Gary: It looks like a dollhouse sitting on a fencepost.

Oh. I thought that was an oversize birdhouse.

Lynn: No, that was our first experiment in being a resource center.

Gary: I built this little building that could hold around 20-30 books. We set it up on that post out front and filled it with old books that we thought people would like. Then we put up a sign saying that anyone could take any book – and anyone could add a book if they so choose. It just sat out there; we didn't have to tend to it.

Lynn: People are doing this all over the country. They call them Little Free Libraries. Look it up online. It's a fascinating little movement. Some of the designs of the houses are adorable.

So you started with the little library. What moved you to start sharing your whole house?

Gary: We're both extroverts.

Lynn: He needs a little more background, dear. As we got to know Nathan and Mathilde and Kyle and Marissa and the others, we saw that they had something our church didn't have.

Gary: We were going to River of Life church. It's a big mega-church with lots of programs and activities and groups.

Lynn: We love the people there.

Gary: We were burned out.

Lynn: It was one campaign after another. Right after we finished one great big volunteer push, another one was underway.

Gary: Sign up for this five-week study, go to our Belize mission trip, volunteer at the crisis pregnancy center, come to this concert, please attend this event, we need helpers for this weekend conference, don't forget to enroll in our evangelism classes, bring your friends to this special outreach event... Yahh! Pastor Hager, he's a great speaker and all, but he kept casting vision after vision after vision. We were neck-deep in vision with no Sabbath in sight.

Lynn: So we dropped out. I know that's horrible, but we did.

It happens to a lot of us.

Lynn: I know, but we really ought to be in some kind of church, you know? How anybody goes through life on their own is just beyond me.

Gary: Anyway, we're extroverts, we're wired to be around people a lot. As these Geneva Two people began to settle in the neighborhood, we discovered that we really liked them. These were people we wanted to be around a lot more.

Lynn: It's just us here; we don't have any children.

Gary: And formally inviting people over as guests is a lot of work. You have to figure out who to invite, what to serve, and how to entertain them while they are here. Work, work, work.

Lynn: It was Gary's insight really. We could have the benefit of having a constant influx of people coming through and none of the hassle of having to plan for them. We can be as sociable as we want. And if we want a little privacy, we simply retreat upstairs to our private rooms.

It sounds like it would be awfully wearing to have all these people trooping through.

Gary: *Laughing,* It probably would be for you! But *we* love it.

Lynn: I think that's the point Gary was making earlier. In the Geneva Two community, we all own private property.

Gary: That's right! We hold to principles of radical sharing, but the application of *how* to radically share is up to us. And if we need to pull back … perhaps to declare a week sabbatical or a month sabbatical, or to pull out of the arrangement, we can do so with no harm, no foul – because everything we offer is a gift, not a mandate.

So this actually works for you?

Lynn: It's not always easy. When we first opened up the resource center, we didn't think to put any limits on the times when people could come in. Some people were over here at midnight and later. That started to be exhausting.

Gary: Exhausting and downright annoying. We're extroverts, but we still need sleep.

Lynn: We should have told the community that we needed to adjust the times our house was open, but we didn't. We simmered and stewed, but we never said anything to anyone. Finally, we came to a breaking point. I'm ashamed to say we didn't handle it very well.

Gary: We handled it fine.

Lynn: Dear, we left for three weeks without telling anyone.

Gary: That's what we always used to do on vacation – it was just hard to adjust to the new responsibility.

Lynn: And you complained about it for the whole first week.

Gary: Not the *whole* week.

Lynn: *She says gently, yet firmly,* Yes, the whole week. And I was as bad as you were. We felt hurt, taken advantage of, and unappreciated, and you know it. *Gary harrumphs.* We even talked about moving to a new neighborhood to escape the mess we'd gotten into. It was really bad.

What turned it around?

Lynn: We came back late on a Sunday night. First thing next day, I received a phone call from Mathilde, asking me out for lunch. Everybody had figured out something was wrong when we disappeared. She wanted to know if we were OK.

And?

Lynn: And I kind of erupted on her. I felt really bad about that.

How did she handle it?

Lynn: She listened. Took it all in. Didn't press me at all. She said that if we had to re-evaluate the roles, that was fine. But she impressed on me that it was very painful for us to run away without confronting the problem. She said that our relationship was far more important to her than the role we played in the community.

And then what happened?

Lynn: I cried, and she cried. It was very embarrassing …
weeping together there at Ground Up Coffee. I don't think that's
how Gary's conversation with the boys went.

Gary: I told Nathan and Kyle how it was going to have to be
if we were going to keep this up.

Lynn: Dear, they also admonished you to set better
boundaries and to learn to communicate your frustrations long
before they got to the breaking point.

So that fixed it?

Lynn: *Laughing,* Oh no. Of course there was this initial
release of tension, but then there were weeks of awkwardness.
Isn't that how it always is after a major confrontation? You build
it in your mind as something terrible, so when it finally comes you
feel great relief. But afterwards there is this time of rawness –
trying to figure out where you stand with the others, wondering if
reconciliation has really happened. Asking yourself, 'Are we still
OK?' On top of that, I was increasingly aware of my own bad
behavior in the process. And that's never fun.

What bad behavior?

Lynn: I had honestly been terrible. I didn't realize how
much I'd been complaining about all these people trooping in and
out of the house. It had been going on for a long time.

A few days after Mathilde and I talked, I was doing my
morning Bible reading: I was at the story of Jesus in the home of
Mary and Martha. That's where Jesus is teaching, Mary is listening
to Jesus and Martha's doing all the cleaning. Martha gets upset
and speaks to Jesus, asking Him to tell Mary to help. Jesus says
that Martha is careful and troubled about many things, but Mary
has chosen the one good thing and that will not be taken away
from her.

To tell you the truth, that story has always annoyed me. I
never liked the idea that the Bible encouraged loafing about. I was

sitting there in the early morning hour, my cup of coffee by my side, the smell of bacon and eggs wafting from the kitchen. Gary was clanking about getting breakfast ready; he was whistling a beautiful tune – that's one of the things that first drew me to him, the way he whistles when he's lost in his work. *Lynn reaches over to pat Gary's hand. Gary bows his head slightly, grins, and places his other hand on hers.* In that moment, I was being joyfully served. Yet somehow, when I was serving others, I lacked joy.

The Holy Spirit pressed this insight on me: Martha's problem was not that she had to serve while Mary learned. Martha's problem was that she wasn't serving with a happy heart. She was doing her work for the sake of the work, rather than doing her work for Jesus. Service with a bitter heart is not service at all, but selfishness.

Gary has been unusually quiet during this story. He speaks now, but without the bluster I've seen before. He almost has tears in his eyes.

Gary: A lot of people of our generation have the idea that living the Christian faith is about striving – constantly working harder and harder. We believe that Jesus died to save us from our sins. But we also get this crazy notion that we need to prove our salvation by working. We think that for Jesus to like us, we had better sacrifice and that sacrifice had better hurt. *Gary pauses and takes a deep breath.*

Lynn and I had to learn that the ability to sacrifice is a grace given to us. Not only are we saved by grace, but we're also made good by grace. The process that God uses to make us good is slow and painful.

We felt this need to over-sacrifice because deep within we wanted to look like spiritual superstars. Then we hit the wall. Our patience came to an end, and we revealed the pettiness lurking in our hearts.

Lynn: It took weeks for us to admit that we had behaved badly. We had a lot of repenting to do before God, and some relationship repair to do among our friends. All I can say is that God changed our hearts. I've been a Christian all my life, and God still had to change my heart.

After that, we learned how to set ground rules that we could live with. We learned how to make the sacrifice with joy rather than through clenched teeth.

Gary and Lynn and I talk much longer about favorite books. We talk about generational differences and about places we have travelled. It is late in the afternoon when I excuse myself. As I drive off, they stand on the front porch and wave goodbye, as though I were their son going off to college.

Judith Peters

I met Judith Peters at the Poiema Furnishings workshop, located in the Oakley business district. The neighborhood, a magnet for fashionable and confident young professionals, is anchored by ultramodern interior design shops, art studios, and locally-run casual gourmet restaurants. This environment has also become an incubator for businesses specializing in niche crafts: hand crafted shoes, artisan hand-sown jeans, traditional letter-press printing, and even a microbrewery.

Nathan Probisco founded Poiema Furnishings in 1998. In his business, he combines a love of well-designed furniture with a sense of environmental responsibility. Most of the pieces that Poiema produces are made from antique wood, reclaimed from old houses. The business has grown alongside of Nathan's other project, Geneva Two.

Judith, a designer and woodworker at Poiema, also lives in the Geneva Two community. After touring the workshop, we sit in the showroom for our interview.

That coffee table – is it a starship?

Right you are. From a certain popular 1960s TV show. Notice how the glass top is cut in the shape of the uniform insignia?

There's got to be a story behind this piece.

Laughing. So there was this uber-wealthy tech millionaire in North Carolina. He saw a magazine article about the movement toward reclaimed wood furniture. It featured a swivel chair that Nathan had designed – a really clever piece, fashioned out of a single reclaimed piece of mahogany. Beautiful work. Apparently this millionaire liked the look. So he called up and commissioned this table.

It was a real design challenge. Hollywood starships are not made with gravity and furniture stability in mind. We had to figure out how to keep the sleekness of the lines and at the same time have the table be functional. Then it took us some doing to find the right woods. We settled on this sweet combination of walnut and teak with cherry used for accents. The customer is driving up next week to pick it up.

I don't even want to know how much this would retail for, do I?

No, you don't. But price isn't a deterrent to dedicated fans. Herb, our office manager, tells us that he expects orders for at least five more when the photos hit the fan websites. We're already setting aside pieces for the rush.

Fascinating, captain. So, if you don't mind my asking, isn't it a little unusual to be a woman in this field?

She shrugs. My Dad kept a woodshop – a hobby that helped him get away from the office, you know? I used to sit on a stool there, watching him work. I loved everything about it, really: the smell and spray of sawdust, the silkiness of finely sanded hardwood. Each saw sang its own pitch, as though it were a monastic chant. When I work in the shop here, I feel like Dad's right with me.

By the time I was in high school, I was making stuff: a guitar stand for my boyfriend, a jewelry box, special signs for my room. When I went to college, I wanted to keep working with wood. So, I worked in the scene shop for the university theater. That was a great experience. I didn't realize it at the time, but I was learning about the practicalities of design: how to conceive of a visual idea; the challenge of executing the concept with the materials at hand; the absolute constraints of time and budget. It would all play right into what I'm doing now.

So it was a natural transition straight into furniture making?

Ironically, no. I never considered working with wood as a career. Dad was in finance – I studied finance. After college, I moved up here to take an entry-level job at Morris Investments in their operations office.

Why did you change careers, then?

I hated it. Imagine spending all day in a four-by-six-foot cubicle, fielding calls from customer service reps, and coding the system to print ad hoc reports for their client support work. It was like I was a pawn being ground down to fit on somebody else's chessboard. After a couple of years, I couldn't take it anymore.

The epiphany came while I was on a Habitat for Humanity blitz build down in the Appalachian Mountains. All I can say is that when I left for that week, I was miserable in my job; by the time I came back … well, let me put it this way: Kyle Edmonds talks about the 'inner compass' as a way the Holy Spirit nudges us toward a calling. When I got back, my inner compass was pointing to wood and saws and stain and glue. I knew that I *had* to make a change.

And how did you get on board with Poiema Furnishings?

It was a natural fit. When I had first moved to the area, I took a room in the Single Sisters House. I thought the Geneva Community was a gift - something exciting and new to be a part of. I've been a Christian all my life; I grew up in the church, and I kind of know the routine of churches. Geneva Two struck me as a really cool and different way of doing church, you know?

How so?

Well, first there is the idea of living in community. A lot of churches function like clubs rather than communities. You join, you go to the events that meet your needs, the paid staff takes care of things. If you're not satisfied, it's easy to drift away.

Geneva is different. We're all there in the same neighborhood, and we're in each other's lives. It's kind of like dorm life, in a way. Only it's more … intense, you know?

Anyway, living in the community is what gave me the opportunity to get on board with Poiema. You know how Gary Chambliss opens up his garage shop for the community to use? Well, I was over there working on some curio cabinets. They were going to be Christmas gifts for my family. Nathan dropped by the house to pick up a book, and he poked his head in the shop. We started talking about craftsmanship; he gave me some pointers. Every little project after that, I would consult with Nathan. He liked my designs, and he gave me great ideas for improvement.

You remember that Habitat trip I mentioned? Well, it was only natural that when I got back, I went straight to Nathan and asked if we could work something out. I was ready to quit Morris Investments right then. Nathan was happy to have someone experienced come on board. I was jazzed about Nathan's vision for sustainable artisan furniture. And the rest is history.

OK, since you bought into the vision, help me understand why Poiema focuses on using reclaimed wood.

First, you have to remember that Cincinnati has a larger than average stock of hundred-year-old homes. You'd be amazed at the incredible quality of the wood in these places, and you'd be horrified at the waste when these old homes are renovated. For years, priceless hardwoods were torn out and sent straight to landfill so someone could "lighten up" their living room with drywall and a coat of "harvest cream" colored paint. Heartbreaking!

Combine that fact with the growing demand for green and sustainable goods. The market was ready for something like this. We get to salvage and work with great materials; our customers get great works of craftsmanship. We all have the satisfaction of knowing that we've kept something wonderful out of the landfill. Everybody wins.

Nathan feels, and all of us agree, that this approach is simply good stewardship – it's wise management of God's resources. Nathan really impresses upon us that this business exists first and foremost to glorify God, and that one of the ways we do that is through our stewardship of these resources. Yes, we have to make a profit, but profit is not the only goal.

That's pretty unusual in today's working world, isn't it?

It's a universe of difference from what I experienced at Morris Investments. There, I felt as though my identity was being sucked from me. Here, it's as though we're becoming more of what we were made to be. There, I had to keep a close watch on how I talked about my faith. Here, our work is an expression of our faith.

One of Nathan's heroes is William Fry, a 19th-century furniture maker and woodcarver from here in Cincinnati. Fry became so well known in his time that he founded a school to teach his craft – a school that resulted in several taking up the woodcarving trade. He made great art; he passed on his expertise; and he left a legacy that continues today. I think that Nathan hopes someday to have the same kind of impact.

It certainly seems like he's well on the way.

Yeah, and get this. The art museum has a room devoted to William Fry's work. There, you can see a portrait of Mr. Fry painted by Frank Duveneck. What's really interesting is that Fry himself designed the frame for that portrait. At the bottom of the frame, he carved into the wood the Latin phrase "Ora et Labora." It translates to "Prayer and Work."

The idea is that prayer and work go hand in glove. We should approach prayer with the seriousness of work, and we should approach our work with the reverence of prayer.

Nathan has taken "Ora et Labora" as his own motto. He impresses upon us that each piece of furniture is a new opportunity to praise God. Our designs are meant to be functional and beautiful as an expression of praise to God. When we select materials, we pay attention to how each piece of wood glorifies God in its own way.

Help me understand that better. How is God glorified by wood?

OK. It's like each piece of wood sings its own song, its own hymn. Oak is sturdy and strong. Pine is porous and flexible. They are different, and in their differences, they bring glory to God. It's my job to know my materials – to know the virtues and limitations of the vast breadth of woods available to us. It's my job to put those different materials in positions where their songs of praise are clear, and where their voices can combine into something greater.

But the idea doesn't stop there. We could be even more specific and say that each *piece* of wood has its own distinctive traits and qualities. One board of pine is different from another in the placement of the knots, the grain of the wood, the warp, even the shade of color that it has taken on as it aged. Nathan has been teaching me to showcase these qualities. That's the true dividing line between craft and art. Craft assembles the materials according to a set plan – art seeks to call forth the voice from the materials and adjusts the design so the materials can glorify God all the more.

It sounds like the shop is very theologically oriented...

Nathan tries to work it that way. He sees his life as a unified whole. His shop, his community, his family – they are all a part of his personal ministry. He really inspires me.

So what are some of the other ways that ministry mindset works out?

Well, one thing he did early on was to provide health insurance for all of us. He didn't have to, and it cost him a lot of money, but he strongly believed it was the right thing to do.

But you might find this more interesting – Nathan provides lunch for everyone in the shop three days a week. I'm not saying he orders a bunch of pizzas or sub sandwiches. Nathan has a caterer come in and prepare healthy and nourishing soups and salads and hearty breads. He decided that he wouldn't feed his employees anything that he didn't want his own family to eat.

He pays for this all out of his own pocket?

Well, yeah. But we all chip in to one degree or another. The chef, Minnie is her name, is launching her own catering business. She uses us as a test kitchen, in a way. Nathan pays her pretty well, but we also have a tip jar that we all contribute to.

Is Minnie a part of Geneva Two?

Oh no, she's a member over at Ebenezer Missionary Baptist. She has come to our monthly gatherings once or twice, and that has led to some interesting opportunities. Maria Sanchez hired Minnie to teach a few cooking workshops for the open house days they have out at Geneva Farms: more customers for the farm, more potential catering clients for Minnie.

I guess that's a real example of why I like working here. Nathan has this intention to bless. And when he blesses, it's like there's a ripple effect, you know? Nathan decides to feed his employees, and that act of kindness leads to more kindness and more opportunity and more blessing. I'll take that over the cubicle archipelago any day.

Hendon McSweeny

Hendon McSweeny is the pastor of "Zoe: a Christian Community Gathered in Cincinnati," the church formerly known as Trinity Presbyterian Church. This is the congregation that gave birth to the original Geneva Two community.

We meet at a Lodestone coffee shop near the church. McSweeny says he keeps his "branch offices" in coffee shops all over the city. In his skinny jeans and black, wrinkle-free mock turtleneck, he looks more the Silicon Valley executive than the Ohio River Valley pastor. As he talks, he gestures and bounces in his seat as though he's been filling up on espresso all day. I spy a hint of a tattoo peeking out from his pushed-up sleeve.

So, tell me about your ink.

He pushes his sleeve farther up his arm to reveal two Asian characters separated by a stylized cross. This first character is the Chinese symbol for "danger" and the second is the symbol for "opportunity." Together they form the word "crisis." A friend of mine in seminary had this same design. He had a really cool story behind it – all about this crisis in his life that brought him to God. I thought it would make a great talking point, so I got one too. You see, there's this crisis point in our lives, when we hit rock bottom. And that's the point where Jesus shows up to work miracles. This tattoo alone has opened the door for me to talk about Jesus with hundreds of people.

Some might think that is a bit contrived – getting a tattoo just to have a talking point. Doesn't it lose some authenticity?

Paul talked about becoming all things to all people so that he might win some. That's all I'm doing. Since I've come here, our community has grown to 600 members. Hard to argue with results, don't you think?

And what have you done as a pastor to make that growth happen?

First, you've got to know that I don't call myself "pastor" – a pastor is an old guy who wears a collar and has tea with dainty little ladies. I call myself a "Social Architect." You see, we're built together as the body of Christ, a living Temple – so how we live our lives together as a community is an expression of that Temple. My job is to guide the direction and building of the beams, frame in the walls, and be champion of the architectural designs. So I cast vision and facilitate community. Then, together we all build this expression of the body of Christ that we call Zoe.

Right. So as "Social Architect," you came in and made some changes to the church.

Sure. The branding of the church was totally dated. I knew within the first month we had to do a total relaunch. After all, I could meet someone here in Lodestar, and they could be really cool and interesting people who are creative and spiritually questioning. Then I'd invite them to church, and they would be totally turned off by the name itself – Trinity – what is that? Presbyterian, I can't even spell that. What does it mean? Too much jargon and religious speak.

And you think "Zoe" is more clear?

Zoe is the Greek word for life. In Jesus we have life and have it abundantly. So there's some mystery in the name, but there's deep meaning as well.

Well, that certainly clears things up...

We had to rebrand in other ways too. We ditched the baby boom rock band for an edgier sound – though now we're starting to experiment with a mix of ancient and future. Our band has been mining the great hymns of the past and setting them to a more upbeat tempo. Right now, they're leaning toward a more acoustic, unplugged sound. People are really responding well.

My most radical idea got some real pushback, though. We took out all the pews from our gathering space and replaced them with dozens of round tables and chairs. As I teach, we give the table groups opportunities to interact and share insights and applications around the table. When social media came on the scene, we installed a screen and began to project the church's hashtag live while I'm delivering the message. As I'm talking, the congregation is responding in small 140 character bursts, and I have the freedom to interact with them as I teach. So the worship gathering has become this interesting and dynamic co-created expression of community.

That's a pretty massive change. Tell me about the pushback that you received.

Sure. We lost dozens of members – mostly older folks who didn't want to let go of traditional worship. But, you know, the elders hired me to bring about change. The congregation said that they had a strong sense of calling to reach the community. My predecessor, Pastor Poteat, had done a great job of instilling within the congregation an understanding that the church is sent to the community. But sadly he was never able to take them to the place where they could do real innovative outreach. I think the tragedy of losing his wife and son in a car wreck just sucked him dry, so when he left for sabbatical, he discerned that he wasn't coming back.

The leaders understood – they had a lot of compassion for Pastor Poteat, but they had their own grieving to do, too. He was really well loved, and it hurt the community a lot when he left. The leaders saw that this was a time not only for healing, but for opportunity to move much more boldly in the direction of missional calling. So they brought me in.

How did the Geneva Two group fit into this time of transition after you became pastor?

Social Architect.

Right. "Social Architect."

Well, they left while I was still hammering out the vision for what the church was going to become. So I came here in 2004. For that first year, I focused on building relationships and encouraging outreach and evangelism. That fall, we kicked off our first church wide campaign; we called it the "Strong Life" campaign. Isn't that a great name? I preached a 6-week series on how the grace of Jesus gives us the strength to live authentically. We encouraged everyone in the church to join a small group. Each group worked through a curriculum that I developed. God did some powerful stuff through that campaign. Lives were really changed.

Just as an aside, these yearly campaigns have been crucial to our success. Every year, people bring friends. I target these messages to be relevant to the life struggles and issues that people face. Our momentum has built every year. So, this year, we're calling our campaign "Now What?" Cool, right? This campaign is all about asking good questions rather than assuming that we have all the answers. We have to learn that life and leadership are more about asking good questions than in spitting out our pre-conceived answers.

I couldn't agree more. So, how did this campaign affect the Geneva Two community?

That was the problem. It didn't affect them. They have a tight knit group there. In a way, they were already doing what I'm leading the rest of the church to do. They were getting to know people in their neighborhood and loving them with a commitment that I pray our congregation members develop. Believe me, I think they're doing great work in that community.

The problem was that they weren't committed to participating in the larger church. Sure, they were members in good standing. Most of them attended worship on Sunday and gave money and volunteered from time to time. But here's what frosted me: they never brought any of the people they were reaching to come be a part of our church. They had several people in their neighborhood that actually joined their community, but never came to church here.

Here's another problem: they let a guy like Alan Gasque be leader in the community. Now, I don't have a problem with Alan personally; as far as I know, he's a committed Christian. You certainly can't deny that he's a powerful personality and gifted at mentoring young men, helping them get direction in their lives. But I'll tell you this: Alan Gasque does not know how to submit to authority. I'm not the guy to tell you that you have to get in line with everything I say, but I at least want some kind of commitment to the church. Alan refused to join. He wouldn't come under the authority of our elders.

Why is that important?

Every spiritual leader needs accountability; otherwise, he runs the danger of becoming a narcissistic monster. I have a Board of Elders who are elected by the congregation; I answer to them and they to me. I'm also accountable to other ministers in the area, and they, in turn, are accountable to me. Let's say one of my colleagues starts abusively pressing people for money or becomes overly controlling in the lives of church members. It is my responsibility, along with our other colleagues, to step in and bring things under control.

So it's a check and balance.

Right. Accountability may be inconvenient, but it protects against a winsome, strong personality accruing so much power and authority that he can't be questioned. It's far too easy to build frightening cults of personalities. The egregious forms you see on TV are the most blatant examples, but it happens in subtler ways, too. We had an independent church pastor here in Cincinnati who controlled all the finances of his church. For decades, he embezzled funds and blew it all gambling at the racetrack.

The long and short is that people – even pastors – are sinful beings, and we need to build structures that restrain our tendency to be selfish. Yes, the Holy Spirit is sanctifying us, but we ought to help in that work by keeping an eye on one another.

And the Geneva Two Group refused that kind of accountability?

Well, Alan Gasque certainly did – at least from me and our elders. I think Nathan is the only person who really can make him see reason. Nathan is really gentle, but he's got a powerfully persuasive way about him. I guess you could call him a born peacemaker, and he's certainly the heart and soul of Geneva Two. He's the only person I know who could bring two bull-headed people like Alan Gasque and Jake Hoffecker into the same group and hold it together for a while. Talk about your two strong and diametrically opposed personalities.

But Jake Hoffecker left Geneva Two...

Sure, but it's a miracle that Nathan held everything together as long as he did. I kept telling him that Jake was a narrow-minded troublemaker. I told him that they needed to ask Jake to leave Geneva Two, but Nathan was so committed to the idea of being a covenanted community that he just wouldn't do it. You'll notice, however, that it was after Jake left that Geneva Two really took off and started to grow. It's really hard for me to not gloat about that fact when Nathan and I talk.

So you keep in touch with Nathan, then?

That was part of our arrangement. We didn't want to unceremoniously cut off relationship with these people – they're doing really good stuff. Living in intentional community is not a life that I would choose, but I can't deny that what they are doing is honoring to God. Honestly, I thank God that there are groups like Geneva Two out there.

Even though they left?

I feel hurt any time someone leaves our church. But this group left for the right reason.

Explain....

Sometimes people leave because they're put out. They've got their knickers in a twist because you've changed the carpet or you didn't pay them enough attention or you offended them by something you said on Sunday. That's a petty, "I'm taking my toys and going home" kind of leaving, and I have no patience for it. As far as I'm concerned, don't let the door hit your bum on the way out.

That's a little harsh.

Well sure, but think about it. Would you put up with that behavior at work or in your family or with your friends? No, you'd say, "Get over it," or you'd have a laugh and move on.

But the church has been infected with this consumer mentality that treats me like I'm a dispenser of religious goods and services for customers who graciously attend. If the all-powerful customer suddenly stops feeling like his needs are met, then he shops in the religious marketplace for a better deal, a newer and fresher model.

That's not church – church is a gathering of God's people who are called on a mission. The church's job isn't about meeting your needs. Only Jesus can fully meet your needs, and sometimes, he does that by changing your understanding of what you need, or even by changing you. He might meet those needs by breaking your heart until you're easier to please. Jesus might meet your needs by letting you weep until you let go of resentment. He might put you in a position to grow in patience while you receive worship music that's really not to your tastes.

He might withhold public acknowledgement of your many works because you need to grow in humility.

No, the church is not in the business of meeting your needs because you don't even really know what your needs are. "My needs aren't being met" is a lousy reason to leave a church.

Then what is a *good* reason to leave?

When you become absolutely convinced that God's calling on your life is taking you on a different trajectory than God's calling for that community. Make no mistake; you should not come to that kind of decision lightly. The Holy Spirit works on us through deep feelings of inward calling, but those feelings are confirmed through the wise counsel of friends and the diligent study of God's word. Eventually, you get this emerging sense of what God would have you do – how God would have you minister to those around you. If that doesn't connect in some way with the congregation of which you are a part, then perhaps God is calling you to another church.

What do you do then?

The Geneva Two situation forced us to ask that very question. It was a tough time for me. We already had people who had left, and more were on their way out. I was already anxious about the congregation shrinking.

The vision of community that Nathan and Kyle worked up was a good and godly vision, but I had to admit that there was no way to make it fit our vision for Zoe. It was clear to me that we were on two completely different trajectories.

You mention Nathan and Kyle … what about Jake?

Like I said, I knew Jake was trouble from the start. I could see that his vision was totally different from that of Nathan and Kyle. I don't doubt that Jake loves Jesus, but he's so narrow. And he was getting narrower as he went along. Jake's idea of community is to gather together and vote people off the island.

And that's not what you did in asking Geneva Two to leave?

Absolutely not! First of all, it wasn't just me asking them to leave. We came to a mutual agreement that this was best. Secondly, we at Zoe wanted to bless Geneva Two and say that they were doing a good work. We wanted to affirm that it's OK for us to be two separate organizations. It's always good to birth something new that becomes its own self-sustaining thing. That's the difference. Jake's mindset is that if you're not with him, then you're not really doing God's work. Our church's mindset, or at least *my* mindset, is that we may not be able to be part of the same organization, but we're still working to build the same kingdom.

And so how did you bless and release the Geneva Two community?

We held a special worship service – a commissioning of sorts. And we continue to have friendships and connections. I'm part of an advisory panel that meets regularly with Nathan and Kyle to talk with them and keep them accountable. It's a lot looser than the kind of controls that I have in my ministry, but at least it's something. So long as Nathan is the *de facto* leader of Geneva Two, I don't worry about the community.

And if he leaves?

Well, there's the problem, isn't it? Right now, it's held together by his personality. And Nathan Probiscos are few and far between. His biggest challenge is to figure out how to build sustainability into Geneva Two, if that's even what he wants.

The Geneva Two Compact January 2006

We, the undersigned, compact ourselves to a Christian covenant community, guided by the Westminster Standards as our locus of doctrinal agreement. As such a covenant community, we hold the following principles.

1. We are not <u>utopian</u>. Humanity is stained and deeply flawed, even more so than we care to admit. This stain affects all our physical, emotional, and mental faculties. As such, we recognize that systems cannot perfect us. We have the capacity to pervert any system, no matter how well designed. Human sinfulness twists even the best systems toward coercion, oppression, and the crushing of others.

2. We are not <u>dystopian</u>. Humans bear the dignity of the image of God. By grace, God renews us and places the Holy Spirit within us. The Holy Spirit teaches, corrects, guides, grows, and makes manifest the goodness for which we were made.

3. Thus, we are **Romantic Realists**. We realistically confront the fundamental brokenness of the world, but we romantically see the purposefulness, beauty, and redemption that God is working and will bring to completion.

4. We are not <u>collectivists</u>. Human society is not well served by having all things in common in a collective sense. We believe God has given stewardship of particular things and particular gifts to particular people.

5. We are not <u>individualists</u>. Human society is not well served by having individuals ruthlessly compete in the pitiless arena of survival of the fittest, for inevitably that will lead to greater oppression, cruelty, and suffering.

6. Thus we are **Covenanted Stewards**. We recognize that we are given individual responsibilities, but we are also made for co-operative society. Our possessions are our own, but they are given to us so that we may be God's instruments of blessing to others.

7. We are not <u>isolationists</u>. God has not abandoned the world, but is instead on the mission to glorify Himself within the world.

8. We are not <u>Constantinian</u>. God has not commanded us to conquer with a sword, nor has He called us to use the mechanisms of power and control to impose our faith on an otherwise pagan society.

9. Thus we are **Culture Creators**. God has given us a mandate to build godly culture. Jesus sends his people to be salt and light to broken humanity. We believe that Christians are to pursue truth, goodness, and beauty in the public sphere of a larger world. In such a way will God be glorified.

Guided by these doctrines and principles, we make the following commitments to one another:

1. We will live in physical proximity to one another, defined as being within a 10-15 minute walk of one another, ideally living in the same neighborhood.

2. We will generously share our resources with one another. We prefer to lend and borrow rather than to get and to spend.

3. We will encourage one another in simplicity, creating a balancing voice against consumerism rampant in our culture.

4. We will show the beauty of the Lord by encouraging one another in creativity, striving to actively create rather than passively consume.

5. We will encourage one another to show the goodness of Christ by being a blessing to the broader community in creative ways.

6. We will encourage one another to grow in the truth of God by attending to the regular teaching of the Word, observation of the sacraments, and the exercise of gentle and gracious admonition.

7. We will regularly and generously give of our financial resources, contributing to a common benevolence fund through which we as a community can bless the frail, the needy, and the marginalized.

8. We will elect wise and spiritually mature elders who will guide the community, teach the word, resolve conflicts, and administer our benevolence giving. If the community wishes, we can authorize these elders to hire a teaching elder to serve the needs of this community.

9. We will regularly and transparently submit our community to examination by outside authorities (of a church denomination or some other oversight group) to ensure that we do not become a cult.

10. When the community reaches 100 members (total adults and children), we will begin the process of exploring future options (which must be enacted by the time the community reaches 150). These options may include (but are not limited to) a. disbanding b. incorporating into a traditional church c. organically dividing into 2 Geneva

Two communities (or other kind of intentional community) d. a group relocating to a distant enough place to start a new Geneva Two community (or other kind of intentional community).

Ray Foster

I meet Ray Foster in his downtown loft. The dominant feature of the sparsely-furnished, high-ceilinged great room is the solid-wood shelving units holding Ray's impressive collection of vintage vinyl records. We sit in comfortable Windsor chairs around a coffee table made from antique wood. I ask if any of the furniture is from Poiema Furnishings – Ray proudly tells me that all of it is.

Ray is a designer with Strang and Company, a product design firm headquartered in downtown Cincinnati. He lived in the Single Brothers House from 2006-2009. Last year, he and a few others moved out of Geneva Two to start a daughter community downtown. The formal title of this community is Finkenwald, after Dietrich Bonhoeffer's underground seminary in Germany. However, to pay homage to their roots, they commonly call themselves Geneva Three.

What was wrong with Geneva Two to make you move out?

Whoa there, let's be clear on this. I didn't just "move out," and neither did the rest of the Finkenwald core group. You've got to remember that part of the vision of Geneva Two was to establish new communities – to spread the DNA of the movement.

I don't think that's in the original Geneva Two compact....

Not the original one, but that document was way before my time. The later compact makes it pretty clear that there was a 150 person cap on the community. Most of the Finkenwald core group came in under that compact.

To be honest with you, I was attracted by the idea that this was a community that put limits on its growth.

Why is that? Is growth a bad thing?

Growth isn't a bad thing – but unlimited growth isn't necessarily a great thing. There are a few megachurches around here. They do lots of interesting things, but they are all built around the personality of the pastor. When a mass of cells keeps pursuing unlimited growth in the body, we call that cancer.

Are you trying to say that megachurches are evil, a cancer on society?

Got your attention on that, eh? Listen, the drumbeat in American Christianity for the past 50 years has been to create bigger churches with more programs. Large churches will never go away. But someone needs to articulate a different vision. Someone needs to have the courage to go seek out the pockets of people who are totally turned off by the homogeneity of the megachurch.

But are megachurches evil?

The better question is "are they healthy?"

Well?

Some are …

And?

And I've come to the conclusion that for me to be a healthy Christian, I need to have a lot more intimacy and accountability with fellow believers.

You're avoiding my question, aren't you?

Chuckles softly. Not exactly. I'm trying to help you understand why I was attracted to Geneva Two. They were intentionally pursuing a different way of being church – a way that stressed deep relationships and deep sharing. To preserve that kind of depth, they need to stay a certain size. Relationships take time and effort and tears. It's just impossible to have deep relationships with several hundred people.

So why not limit growth then? Why not just stop allowing new people to join?

Fair question. But Christianity doesn't really work that way, does it? After all, Jesus did say to go and make disciples; that isn't an optional command. It's not really our place to decide that we're comfortable and then stop making new disciples.

And let's just assume that we did stop bringing in new people to our community. Do you know what the fastest growing religious group in America is? The Amish. These are not people who are known for aggressive outreach, and yet because of their high birth rate, they grow at about 5% a year. That doesn't seem like much, but it means they double in size roughly every 20 years. And let's remember, the Amish value small communities, so what do they do when the communities grow too big? A group of Amish heads out to buy new land and start new businesses. I read a news article that estimates that a new Amish community starts every 3 weeks!

So you see, it's really not that radical to want to start new independent communities. In fact, it's really healthy – probably the best way to make sure the DNA of your community continues on.

This is the second time you've said "DNA of the community." What do you mean by that?

In part, that's what the Geneva Compact tries to sum up: the essentials, the deep values that bind the community together. I think if you asked anyone in the community about the DNA, they'd point straight to the compact.

I look at DNA another way: it is found in the types of questions that the community asks. I'm a designer. My job begins with asking great questions. At Strang and Company, we have one little exercise called "seven whys." For any given design challenge, we ask "why" seven times, drilling deeper into the consumer's psyche so that we can learn about their deep needs.

It all just illustrates the need to keep asking, asking, asking questions. And when we're done, ask a few more.

I see what you mean. I'm finding that people in Geneva Two seem to be more interested in asking questions than in pushing answers.

That's right! And what's more, the people of Geneva Two were asking the kinds of questions that really interested me: what is the nature of life together as Christians? Is there a more humane way of living? How do we foster creativity and caring? How do we structure a neighborhood to encourage people to connect, to worship, and to create? Simply put, how do we re-think how to be Christians together?

It's an optimistic vision – something I haven't experienced in many churches. Most of the traditional churches I've been in have been about power and control. They've been about gatekeepers who say "no" to new ideas. Geneva Two is all about possibility and experimentation and personal growth.

OK, I get the DNA piece, and the impulse to create new communities. Why downtown Cincinnati?

The great artistic and intellectual ferment of any age happens on the fringe, in the place of experimentation and radical living. In this city, that would be downtown, or more properly, the Over-the-Rhine neighborhood. It's been an economically depressed neighborhood for decades, riddled with crime, crumbling buildings, and poverty.

That environment draws pioneers – people who don't care for social convention. These people become the opening wave of a transformation of the community. It's a familiar pattern: Greenwich Village in New York, West Cambridge in Boston, Inman Park in Atlanta. Right now in 2010, Over-the-Rhine is starting to experience an influx of pioneers who are smart, creative, highly self-sufficient, and incredibly skeptical. We've got artists and singer/songwriters and professionals and doctoral students and community organizers and poverty-line families who are all part of an eclectic gumbo. It's a vibrant pulsating hub of catastrophic humanity.

Now imagine hacking into that jungle and setting up a Jesus-centered community.

Sounds terrifying ....

It's freaking amazing! Awesome design thrives on awesome challenge. Awesome rewards demand awesome risks. The Geneva Two group took a small risk in doing something different in suburbia. We're taking the kernel of that idea and transplanting it to a different soil. We're ratcheting up the risk to insanity level.

It's insane risk because of the crime and drug dealing?

Kind of, though those risks are overplayed. There is risk of violence everywhere you go. Drug deals happen in the wealthiest suburbs. There are crazy people in any neighborhood.

But really, I'm talking about the emotional risks. The center city is home to a lot of people that simply hate Christians. I don't mean they're foaming at the mouth lunatics. These are nice, interesting, intelligent people I'm talking about. And yet they hate Christians – not personally. mind you, only in the abstract. And only a few would state it so nakedly, but still there's this deep sentiment. So many people, right or wrong, feel angry because the church has wounded them.

Or they resent what they think of as the ignorance of Christians. You get a few loud-mouthed preachers with bad hair and a TV presence, and they can really poison the groundwater for any kind of meaningful ministry. Televangelism and politics have turned too many people against Christianity. People down here think that Christians hate people like them. They came here to get away from the suburbs, which they see as strongholds of conventional morality and Christianity. They ran straight to the center city, where they can live like they please without interference.

And you think you can change that?

Hate fixates on the abstract. It's hard to hate what you know. If we can be involved in the community, be deeply connected in downtown, and yet still maintain our identity as followers of Jesus, then we get an audience. Isn't that what Jesus did? He dined with the prostitutes and the outcasts and the wealthy secular tax collectors. He went to be *with* them. That's what we're trying to do in Finkenwald.

We talk for a long time about Finkenwald and its distinctive emphases. However, since this volume is about Geneva Two, I've opted to omit these additional reflections. Perhaps someday I will come back and do a different story on Finkenwald and the challenges of urban intentional community.

Alan Gasque

With his larger than average build, large biceps, and trim waist, one might confuse Alan Gasque for a professional athlete. He sports a slightly bushy goatee which complements his closely cropped salt-and-pepper hair. We meet at a smoothie bar, where he orders a healthy-sounding concoction containing cucumber, celery, acai berry, and kale, with an added shot of super antioxidant powder. It smells foul, and I struggle to restrain my gag reflex.

Alan emanates the dynamism of a man with immense stores of latent energy. It's not the restless energy that comes out in jiggling legs and tapping hands. Rather, readiness radiates from him, a readiness to bend his full energies and attention to meet whatever challenge rises in his path. Sitting with him, I feel that he is more vibrant, more alive, and more aware of the fullness of the moment than anyone around him. Strangely, I find this feeling both disconcerting and heartening.

What brought you to Geneva Two?

I left teaching back in 1999. Eleventh and Twelfth grade English. I did my time and had a great run, but it was time for me to move on. Teaching is wonderful when you have motivated kids and supportive parents. But I found that each year brought me increasingly spoiled students and parents who treated me as the hired help.

To give you an example: I had one student who blew off class for a whole month. He produced less-than-credible excuses for his failures to turn in assignments. Detentions had no effect. It goes without saying that he failed his midterm. The kid's otherwise absent father called me for a meeting. In this meeting, this mid-level corporate executive had the temerity to tell me that his wastrel son's failure was unacceptable. He demanded to know what I would be doing about it. Apparently I was supposed to fix the grade or give special opportunities for make-up work.

Sounds maddening – how did you handle it?

I told him that his little pride and joy had earned a failing grade. I told him that his son needed to feel the consequences of failure, else he would learn to accept mediocrity. And then I told this blustering fraction of a father that a spoiled son would cause him nothing but sorrow.

A little over the top, don't you think?

Chuckles. He didn't like that too much. Principal Stover said I stepped over the line on that one. He backed me up on the grade, but he suggested that I learn to be 'a tad more diplomatic.'

Well, critiquing a fathers' parenting might not be the best way for a teacher to win friends.

You may be right. But I keep up with a few students from that class. Just for the record, let me tell you the rest of the story: that boy barely squeaked through college, developed a recreational drug habit, impregnated two different women with children he never bothers to see, and continues to be unable to hold down a steady job. He's 33 and lives as a functional dependent on his parents. I might've been harsh, but I was right.

Anyway, I did what I wanted to do with teaching and moved on. I started my own business as a personal trainer and fitness coach.

That's quite a change.

It is, but it isn't. I still help people grow, achieve, and become better. The main difference is that I have an older, more motivated clientele.

An unforeseen advantage is that the fitness profession is quite portable: I can pick up and go anywhere. Every city has people who want to lose weight and get healthy. So when Nathan talked to me about Geneva Two, I was intrigued.

How did you and Nathan know each other?

He was one of my best students: earnest, bright-eyed, a keen and inquisitive mind. Every so often, a student comes along and you say to yourself, "This is one of the good ones." Nathan is one of those. So, I made it a point to keep in touch.

To tell the truth, his vision for Geneva Two didn't surprise me. It was exactly the kind of idealistic thing I would have expected from him. He never had a hint of cynicism. Oh, he could be sarcastic, just like all high school boys. But his sarcasm didn't have that cutting edge. It never occurred to him to use sarcasm as a weapon; it was merely a way to share something he found funny. If anyone would believe that people could live in this kind of intentional community, it would be Nathan.

You sound like you had doubts about the Geneva Two experiment.

Not doubts. No. I guess you could say that if you take that idea of being "Romantic Realists," then I would fall less on the "romantic" side and more on the "realist."

So what about Geneva Two drew you?

The earnestness of it all. They talked about their vision for community like it really *mattered*. Instead of self-protective ironic detachment, these kids demonstrated great humility. These people were pioneers putting their hearts on the line. They all could have had exciting careers that took them to exotic places. They all could have earned six figures and lived in starter castles in the suburbs. Instead they chose to live in a humble city neighborhood and sink roots in the soil here. I suppose I wanted a little piece of that, too.

So you bought a house in the neighborhood. How did it become the Single Brothers House?

I saw a need. Every culture has its typecast for young men: the warrior in ancient Greece, the chivalrous knight in Arthurian Romance, the comic book heroes of the '40s and '50s.

In our culture, young men are cast as idiots. The idea of masculinity that is fed to us in TV and movies is that men are drunken, sex-obsessed slackers who are, for the most part, dim. They may be friendly, but only in a goofy and clueless way. Any amount of irresponsible behavior is excusable so long as you're good-natured and a little lovable. And in the end, this loveable idiot gets the beautiful, smart, and professional girl.

Let me present you with a harsh fact: life doesn't bless the loveable idiot. Life hits him hard and cruelly. He doesn't get the smoking-hot girl. Instead, if he's lucky he might get a shrew, a harridan who resents his childishness and sets about the impossible project of improving him. The lovable idiot earns no respect from his peers or his employer, and in reality, he has no respect for himself. So, beneath his easygoing party-boy exterior is a well of subcutaneous anger. He's angry because he knows he could be so much more. He knows that he's wasting potential. At his core, the loveable idiot is angry because he's deeply disappointed in himself.

That's a pretty harsh diagnosis.

Like I said, I veer more to the "realist" than the "romantic." The reality is this: men who act like boys get treated like boys. And they seethe inside because of it.

So how does Single Brothers House address that problem?

One of my martial arts instructors told me that the best way to control dangerous young men was to have them in the company of dangerous old men. Young men are naturally rough until they get around a tough, experienced, and powerful older man.

And that's you?

I'm as close as they're going to get. The Single Brothers House is a place for me to draw close to young men and show them something better.

So how does it work?

The basic idea is that I offer a very low rental rate – enough for me to cover expenses. I don't need to make a profit on the house; my personal training business covers my financial needs. In exchange for the rental rate, the tenants agree to a formal living contract that spells out their responsibilities. Each tenant agrees to basic things like dividing chores and respecting one another. Nothing too burdensome.

These things really need to be spelled out?

You would be amazed at the boggling level of cluelessness among a certain segment of the population. It's enough to make you fear for the Republic. We have a whole generation that has been coddled – they expect a medal for showing up. So, yes, we have to spell out some basic rules of discipline and respect. We lay out a rotation for cleaning the kitchen, vacuuming the living room, scrubbing the bathroom. Each tenant contributes to a shared fund for household necessities like paper towels, toilet paper, cleaning supplies, etc. Each month, we agree on a number of meals we'll share and who will do the cooking. The mindset of personal responsibility has to be taught to most of these boys.

And they respond?

Some do. Some get mad – those are the ones that usually leave. It's funny, because I'm up-front about expectations. Each applicant goes through an interview process where I thoroughly explain the rules. No one can say they came in not knowing what is expected. And yet the enforcement of agreed-upon expectations makes them mad. "You mean you actually mean for me to *live* this way?"

So the slackers are the ones who leave?

Generally. Though, sometimes it's the opposite. We had one fellow, Andre was his name. He understood self-discipline and self-management. His room was always neat and he went above the call of duty in taking care of things around the house. In a lot of ways, he was a great renter.

But he had no grasp of how to be gracious to others: no patience for fools and no slack for people who weren't holding up their end of the bargain.

Pardon the observation, but you don't seem to suffer fools well either...

Laughs. No, I don't. I've been told that I have a tendency to bulldoze people. I'm aware of that and try to keep it in check. Teaching high school helped me learn how to be happy if someone just *tries* to learn self-discipline. If you want people to learn and grow, you have to meet them where they are. If you teach a dog to play checkers, you don't criticize the game.

Andre had no patience for people being in the process. He had high standards for himself, and if others didn't live up to those standards, he had no respect for them. It was a quiet kind of disdain – withdrawn into himself, not really giving people time to explain themselves.

Eventually, he left and moved into an apartment where he could be alone in his rightness.

Any other particular challenges?

Sure – the crusaders who have all the answers, the swaggering, theology-head reformer boys. They're full of grand visions, and they're ready to take to the streets and show us benighted geezers how things ought to be done. They want to reform society, but they don't even know how to make their bed or mow the yard. How can you fix the problems of America if you can't even balance a checkbook or live within a budget? Go learn how to do your laundry and then maybe we can talk about changing the world.

I understand you added a second house for women?

Right. In 2007, we opened the Single Sisters House. It runs on similar principles: a safe place for young women to figure out how to be confident and responsible in life. But it would be quite inappropriate for me to meddle too much in their lives. I hired Rosalind to live there and run it as a kind of "house mom" – which is funny since she's not that much older than most of the tenants.

How do your tenants relate to the rest of Geneva Two?

It's up to them. But I've rigged the system, in a way. Single Brothers house is smack in the middle of the neighborhood, Single Sisters is right around the corner. And the members of the community are deliberate about getting to know the people who move in. My tenants can't help but build relationships with people in the community. Then the job is half done. The dangerous young men find themselves immersed in a neighborhood full of interesting and dangerous old men.

But it doesn't work for everybody.

No, of course not. Like I said, I have several people move out pretty quickly. I don't make tenants sign a lease – everyone is month-to-month. I want people to have an easy escape if they need it.

That escape clause has helped in another way. We've had a few men decide to buy houses or move out into a nearby apartment so that the community could open up space in Single Brothers. Some of our folks have moved out to be a part of the Geneva Farms experiment. And some others have moved downtown where they're starting another Geneva-like community. No, just because someone leaves, that doesn't mean we've failed. Many times, when one of my tenants leaves, I consider them to have graduated – it's like welcoming them into the civilized world after an apprenticeship. I've got to admit, that's pretty satisfying.

James and Nichelle Han

In 2005, Dr. James Han accepted a position on the staff of Cincinnati Medical College, which brought the Han family from San Francisco to Cincinnati. A mixed race couple (James is Asian-American while Nichelle is African-American), the Hans were wary about moving from the tolerant and fluid society of California to the reputedly stiff, tradition-bound Midwest. Despite her trepidations, Nichelle, also a physician, had no problem securing a position with a family practice.

With two children under the age of five, the Hans keep a surprisingly orderly household. They decorate with the spare modernistic style of sleek furniture on hardwood floors. Their children enjoy playing with carefully selected toys, mostly made from natural materials: wooden puzzles, metal trucks, hand-sewn stuffed dolls, well-loved books, beanbags made from worn-out jeans, a model castle built from cardboard and decorated with hand-colored construction paper. A montage of framed black and white family photographs decorates one wall.

The Hans have invited me for dinner; they serve a light, yet flavorful, vegetarian lasagna made with fresh squash and zucchini from the Community Supported Agriculture program at Geneva Farms. Homemade peach ice cream (made with locally grown organic peaches, cream from free range grass-fed cows, and organic cane sugar) is our dessert.

You found out about Geneva Two before you moved to Cincinnati.

James: Yes. Once we decided we were definitely moving, I started intensive research....

Nichelle: James did more than research. He meticulously cataloged the pros and cons of every neighborhood, and he indexed each community according to driving distance to the hospital and proximity to the major cultural attractions we were interested in: the Art Museum, The Black Box Theater, Music Hall.

James: … and library branches, churches, and grocery stores. Location is everything in home buying, and I quickly discovered that neighborhood is everything in Cincinnati.

You certainly do things diligently, don't you?

James: You want your surgeon to be Type A....

Nichelle: We were giving up a lot, moving here from San Francisco. So, we wanted to make sure that it was going to be the best possible move for us.

When did you start considering the Geneva Two community as a possible home?

James: I mentioned that one of our criteria for home buying was proximity to churches. We're committed Christians, and participating in a church community is important to us. In my research, I found *The Cincinnati Examiner*'s article on Geneva Two. We were immediately interested. I called Kyle Edmonds that day and set up a phone interview.

A phone interview? I've never heard of anyone phone interviewing people in a neighborhood before they move in.

James: Well, intentional community is quite a bit different from simply moving into a neighborhood.

Nichelle: We had to know where they were coming from. What did they believe about God? How rigid were they? We didn't want to find ourselves flirting with some kind of gun-hoarding separatist group.

James: Anyway, the initial conversation with Kyle went well, so when we flew out to look at homes, we planned on staying an extra day, just to spend time with the people in Geneva Two.

Nichelle: We really liked what we saw, even though we perceived an underlying problem.

Problem? What problem did you see?

Nichelle: It was obvious to us that there was a serious rift between Alan and Jake.

And what did you observe about this rift?

James: Jake is basically an extreme nut-job who thinks that America should be a theocracy…

Nichelle: James, that's not fair. Jake wouldn't say that.

James: It's the logical end of his argumentation.

Nichelle: You've got to admit that Jake can be very kind. He's got this boyish earnestness to him that might come across a little strong, but he would never suggest that we outlaw other religions.

James: That's only because he's blind to the implications of his own theology. He wants Cromwell's England … he wants Puritan New England all over again. Throw the dissenters in the stocks and don't spare the rod.

If you had such a problem with Jake, didn't that give you pause about joining Geneva Two?

James: Jake's not part of Geneva Two anymore. By the time we visited the community, Jake had already lost the battle for the long-term vision.

Nichelle: During our visit, Nathan showed us the revisions they were working on for the Geneva Compact. Alan made sure to point out the "We are not Constantinian" language. He wanted to make it clear that the community was intentionally turning away from the seductive idol of political power.

So you understood that to mean the community eschewed politics?

James: No, no, no. You just articulated Jake's critique of the "not Constantinian" language, but that's not what it means. Christianity is a whole-life commitment – politics is a part of it. Jake has a deaf ear for nuance and difference.

Then can you enlighten me to the difference?

James: Constantinianism is a particular way of doing politics – one that has been largely adopted by the Evangelical movement. It asserts that Christians should flex their political muscles and operate the levers of power in our democratic republic.

Since the culture wars of the '70s and '80s, this approach has focused on advancing a particular legislative agenda. However, that pursuit of political influence has led to dirty deals, power-lust, and win/lose relationships with the rest of the world.

The worst part is that this emphasis on power has seduced Christians into the exaltation of swaggering, glib-tongued pastor-boys who beat the drums of the culture wars. We Christians mistake anger for passion and confuse volume with conviction. We would rather sit under leaders who whip up an exciting show of fear than heed the shepherds who warn us of the logs in our eyes.

Nichelle: The fallout in California is really bad. The culture-war mindset has completely alienated a whole generation.

James: In trying to win little political battles, Christians have essentially told a lot of people to go to Hell.

Nichelle: James....

James: Well, it's true.

OK, but the question is still out there – how is "not Constantinian" something other than a complete withdrawal from politics?

James: First of all, both Peter and Paul tell us that we have to "honor the emperor." In our democratic republic, the "emperor" is the electorate, the citizens. Citizenship in our country isn't simply about rights; it's also about responsibilities. That includes a responsibility to participate in politics. So, biblically, we can't justifiably withdraw and be uninvolved.

Nichelle: James, that's not really getting at what he's asking. Let me try shedding some light here with a different question:

Why are ideological positions the starting place for how Christians engage in politics?

OK, I'm not sure where you're going with this...

Nichelle: Right now, Christians spend the bulk of their energy advocating for particular ideological positions. To be a Christian is to be "for this" or "against that." And any kind of nastiness is justified to advance the ideological cause

I'm with you so far...

Nichelle: But Christians are supposed to demonstrate the fruit of the Spirit in their character, right? Love, joy, peace, patience, kindness, goodness, faithfulness, gentleness, and self-control – all those virtues listed in Galatians.

Still with you.

Nichelle: So what if instead of focusing on ideological purity, we focused on making sure that our *conversations* about politics reflect the Biblical fruit of the Spirit? What would it look like if Christians showed the goodness of Christ in the *way* in which they engaged in politics? What if we strove to reflect peace and patience and gentleness and kindness in our political speech?

James: How about this – what if we trusted God's sovereignty so much that we didn't have to cast our political opponents as traitors, addled in the brain, or nefarious? We could stop with the character assassinations and ridiculous tearing down of our political opponents. After all, governing isn't a chess game in which "our side" is supposed to win at all costs. An honest and vigorous debate does not mean we have to deny our opponent's right to hold an opposing view.

Nichelle: What could we accomplish if we redirected the energy that Christians exhaust in lobbying, rallying the troops, and fighting national political battles? Imagine if even half of that money, time, and organizational skill were spent on promoting projects in which we believe?

Then your approach to politics is just to talk differently about it?

James: Not just talk differently, but also speak from a place of humility. Culture warriors take a stance of certainty as they apply the Bible to public policy in contemporary America. Don't get me wrong, I believe the Bible is true and that the main things are quite clear. That said, when we're looking at a text from the world of ancient empires and applying it in a modern democratic republic, we've got to make a few leaps of abstraction. We've got to ask questions that most of the ancients didn't have to ask.

For instance?

James: Our republic is founded on several principles, including securing maximum liberty. So, how much do we allow people the liberty to do sinful things?

Take speech for instance. The ancient Israelites didn't have a constitutional guarantee of freedom of speech while they were subject to the Babylonians or to the Romans. We have such a guarantee.

The Bible has a lot to say about how we as *individual Christians* are to regulate our own speech. Jesus makes it pretty clear in the Sermon on the Mount that we aren't supposed to destroy people with our words. And if his teaching isn't clear enough, then the book of James makes it abundantly clear – insults, cruel barbs, denigrating comments are all, at their root, sinful.

However the Bible tells us nothing about how to enact laws that honor the principle of the freedom of speech for *all people* in a society. At least it doesn't tell us anything *directly*. We have to search the scriptures, prayerfully discern underlying principles, and humbly make application, realizing that in doing so we're walking the high wire without a net.

In other words, the question of "how do I live" as a Christian is quite different from "how do we allow others to live…"

James: Exactly.

Are there other questions, then?

James: Sure, what is the proper role of the different levels in our system? The American government was designed with a separation of powers at the federal level, and was intended to foster robust and locally-run state and municipal governments. Our system is supposed to distribute power among many different parties, and it was built that way because humans are not angels. So before riding off on some shining-teeth televangelist's crusade to petition the President to ban movies about fast cars and faster women, it behooves us to ask, "is this issue really the President's job?"

So how does this different approach to politics play out in Geneva Two?

James: Well, we ultimately all agree that while political involvement is a responsibility of the Christian, our hope does not lie in politics.

Can you tease that out for me then?

Nichelle: Let me see if I can shed some light. Jesus is our Lord and our King. Our main hope is not in the advancement of a particular party, candidate, or agenda. Our hope is in Jesus, first and foremost. We don't pin our hopes on politics. That ordering of things helps us stay peaceful; it takes the emotional edge off political conversations. We might be disappointed by election results, but we are never devastated because we don't hang that much hope on them to begin with.

James: You know, the members of the early church were political losers for three hundred years of Roman persecutions. Christians are generally political losers under the crescent of Islam.

Russian Christians were political losers under the atheistic Soviet Union. If all those Christians could all hold up their heads and say, "I will wait upon the Lord to renew my strength," then I think that maybe American Christians, who by the way enjoy the greatest freedom in the world, can lose an occasional election and not think the Antichrist has arrived.

Nichelle: May I turn the conversation in a slightly different direction?

I'm all ears…

Nichelle: I would also add that a deep hope in Jesus also gives us the perspective to see that our role in society is a lot bigger than simply acting as political creatures.

OK, I'm interested. Carry on.

Nichelle: Creating culture. That was one of the commitments that attracted us to Geneva Two.

James: Right! Alexis de Tocqueville, in *Democracy in America*, talks about the voluntary associations in America. Most of the work of building society gets done by ordinary citizens who band together to make good things happen. Our political system was designed –

Nichelle: James, give it a rest. We're off politics for now.

James: I was just –

Nichelle: *Sternly*. James!

James: Sorry. Go on.

Nichelle: Well, this community values people who don't wait around for someone else to make things happen. We don't sit around saying "there oughtta be a law" or gripe to one another about how "somebody needs to do something."

For example – when there was a rash of car break-ins last year, Alan took it on himself to organize a neighborhood watch program. And when Mrs. Van Doehrn's house is looking a little run down, we don't call Senior Services. Instead, Nathan goes over with a paint crew.

Or look at the businesses that are borne out of this community: Poiema Furnishing, Geneva Farms, the Single Brothers and Sisters Houses – why even Jake's mail order book business (*James snorts, but says nothing*). These organizations shape our community more than any amount of hard-charging political activity.

So you're saying that the people of Geneva Two are still activists, but of a different sort?

Nichelle: That's a great way of phrasing it. To be a Christian is to be active. While some churches encourage their members to be political activists, we were strongly attracted to this community because they shape people to be cultural activists. I think, after all, that's what the word "citizen" used to mean.

As we finish our dessert, Nichelle tucks in their two children while James pours glasses of Madeira for us all. The rest of the evening's conversation courses over the arts, educational theory, great books, and food-lover websites. It is midnight before I leave, exhausted and with my brain brimming over with future writing projects.

Gerald Schroeder

Gerard Schroeder fits the stereotype for the modern science fiction writer. He wears his hair just above the shoulders, where it seems to merge with a shaggy beard. Retro-chic Buddy Holly glasses frame his pale grey eyes. As we talk he appears to be practicing a hyperkinetic exercise routine: gesticulating, glancing, tapping his foot, jogging his leg, spinning a pencil about his finger.

He peppers his conversation with more profanity than I expect from a member of the Geneva Two community. This makes capturing his voice difficult, as my editors impose a strict no-profanity policy. To preserve something of the flavor of Gerard's conversation, I've transcribed offensive words into profanitype – the meaningless string of ancillary keyboard characters that comic strips use. I leave the reader to mine her imagination in translating these phrases.

We meet at Ground Up Coffee. He's been waiting for me, and it appears that he's already drained two or three mugs before I arrived.

Gerald, pleasure to meet you. I enjoyed your novel *Singularity's Child.*

Gerald throws his hands up in the air. What, you haven't read *Dr. Fausto's Cabinet of Curiosities?* Well only about twelve people read that one. *He laughs.* Seriously, thanks so much for reading; I'm grateful when someone enjoys any of my work.

What's next, then?

Well, I'm done with the sequel to *Singularity's Child.* We're waiting on the cover art now – the publisher switched artists. *Singularity's Child* got great reviews, but people said the cover looked like it was for a bad romance novel. The *Balrog Lair* blog awarded it "Best Book with a Bad Cover."

How do people respond to you as a Christian writer?

First of all, get it right. I am not a "Christian" writer. *Gerald makes quotation mark gestures when he says "Christian." He does this gesture every time "Christian" is used to describe a marketing demographic.* Most of the dreck that's marketed as "Christian" fiction is warmed-over sermon illustrations that have all the staying power of Dollar Store air freshener. I don't write Amish romance and I don't write angel-versus-demon action adventure and I don't do heartwarming tales about fathers rediscovering their sensitive sides.

But you are a writer who is a Christian...

So? I don't write for the "Christian" market. The "Christian" market doesn't have a place for guys like me.

And that means?

Guys who grew up playing *Dungeons and Dragons* and guys who watch *Dr. Who.* Guys who don't identify with sports metaphors or business jargon or anyone who wears clothes from J. Crew. Guys who are gamers, oddballs, spazzes, and geeks. Guys who listen to indie rock and still collect comics, which by the way we don't mind calling comics - #&$% this "graphic novel" &%$#.

I write science fiction. $%&# awesome science fiction, too. My characters operate in a moral universe, and extraordinary things happen to them. My challenge is to make the imaginative world believable. In my worlds, there's sin and there's glory and a lot of &%^&$ up people who happen to also be awesome and amazing and heroic. You can't write these kinds of stories when you have some Sunday school lesson axe to grind.

So how does an up-and-coming science fiction writer come to live in a Christian intentional community?

That is not one of my better stories, and it's a really long one.

I'm game.

OK, then. But hang in there with me. Let's rewind back to how I started to write. I grew up in Columbus. In high school, I was always drafting these little stories, but most of them really sucked. I was just imitating what I liked. So I wrote space opera knock-offs or fantasy tales set in Middle Earth. I tried comedy; I wrote this story about an intergalactic musical revue that sets up shop on Broadway – kind of a social satire on the New York theater scene, but with vaporizers and tentacled aliens.

Sounds ... Interesting.

Yeah. Interesting is my euphemism for "$&*!" too. It was awful. But part of the process is writing through the bad stuff so that you learn to recognize the good stuff when it comes. I've heard it said that it takes 10,000 hours of diligent practice to master any given subject. Well, that story was around 500 hours into my 10,000.

So anyway, in college, I fell in with a writer's group. We were all English Lit majors – this was at DuSable U. up in Chicago. Our weekly meetings were supposedly for reading and critiquing each other's work, but usually we just drank coffee and carped on the literary offenses of John Grisham. We were convinced that for fiction to be good, it had to be abstruse. I wrote this ponderous, 240-page Faulkner knock-off; it only contained three sentences. Gads, we were so pompous! It's embarrassing how full of ourselves we were. We vomited out turgid, overblown prose, and no one ever told us that "less is more" or "clarity trumps cleverness" or "keep it simple, stupid."

The typical college writer's group, then...

Laughs. I knew I liked you for a reason. Now here's the dark truth. We were horrible human beings: brutal and condemnatory and burning inside with rage that we didn't understand. The betrayals and love triangles and gossip and angry fights and drunken reconciliations were exhausting. We were really %&$@*^ up people.

It doesn't sound at all like the life of someone who would join an intentional Christian community.

So here's the peculiar thing: all that time, I thought I was a Christian. I grew up in church, right? I went to youth group and did all the routine. I never abandoned my beliefs, but I sure put them on the back burner. I was living like #$&%, and my faith was hidden away, like a child's beloved toy, tucked away in a box under a blanket of dust in the attic, waiting to be brought out for the next generation. All during that time, my faith lay there, waiting on me, whispering to me, "There is more in heaven and earth than is dreamt of in all your philosophy, Horatio."

So what brought your faith out of the attic and into your life again?

Love. After college, I stayed in Chicago, but I floundered. I wanted nothing to do with a regular corporate job, so I took a gig as a barista in a coffee shop. And that's where I met Annie.

She worked in the same shop, and when we had the same shift, we talked. Annie's a musician, an indie singer/songwriter. She reads good books and talks politics. You would never see her wearing makeup or pretty dresses or girly stuff. She's raw and blunt and iconoclastic. I fell for her, and hard.

Annie is also a seriously committed Christian. Oh, she shared all my critiques of the institutional church: the hypocrisy, the bourgeois sensibilities, the consumer-mindset. But she also had this deep, solid, unwavering confidence. For her, it's all real – all the miracles and salvation and Holy Spirit and Jesus coming back. Faith isn't a compartment in her life – it's the framework that holds it all together and gives it shape.

Looking back, I can only say that God was using Annie to push me up into the attic to re-discover that old faith.

What happened next?

So Annie is a part of this house church. She invites me to visit.

Imagine this scene. I walk in to the living room of this house and it's packed out with about 25 people. Then this tatted-up, shaved-head guy stands up and says, "All right, let's pray." Everyone squints their eyes shut and they all start to pray – first only the leader, but then everyone in the room talking at once. Someone over in the corner starts to jabber in some language unknown to man. And this goes on for twenty minutes or more. Then we sing a bunch of songs that I don't know. And then shaved-head guy gets up again and starts to teach. It was electric and strange and raw. I didn't know whether to run screaming or to take notes for story ideas.

I was hooked. The people in this house church were poor and bohemian and avant-garde. But also clever and smart; they were thinkers. Come to think of it, they weren't all that different in outlook from the people in my college writer's group.

That's not exactly a resounding endorsement, is it?

No, no. That didn't come out right. The interests were similar, but the attitudes were completely different. These people *loved* each other, and they loved in a way I had never experienced. They could be as emotionally messy as anyone in my writer's group, but no one got angry about it. Instead of anger, there was this infectious joy that seemed to bounce back and forth among them. In that joy, they gave each other space, and in that space, some found healing.

That's where I first experienced grace.

Sounds like it was a good season of life for you.

It was glorious. The deeper I got into this church, the more I saw the grime in my soul. And the more I began to experience Jesus cleaning it away. It was a sweet time.

So what happened?

As I was growing, I was also falling harder for Annie. And you know how this story goes. Guy falls in love with the girl.

Girl thinks of the guy as "a brother." Guy pours his heart into the friendship and prays the girl will fall for him. Girl falls for some other guy and wants everyone to be friends. I was living in a John Hughes movie.

The tension was too much; I was becoming a total head case. I had to get out of there. So I moved to Cincinnati.

Just moved? You didn't have any connections or family or prospects for work?

I was reacting, not planning. I'd fallen for Annie badly – I swear I was crazy mad in love with her. The ache built inside until I felt I would burst. I couldn't take that &^%$ any more, so I got the &$^% out of Dodge.

Cincinnati was a lot closer to home, but still far enough away, if you get what I mean. And believe it or not, there's this great creative scene here: independent theater, local music, writers' groups, art galleries, microbrews, hacker collectives. What better place to cultivate my craft?

So when you moved, you came straight to Single Brothers House?

No. I found an apartment downtown – this was back before downtown became the go-to neighborhood. But I had a hard time finding a church. I visited a few places, but they were nothing like I'd experienced in Chicago. So I did a web search on "Cincinnati house church" and boom, I came across Geneva Two. When my lease at the downtown apartment was up, I moved in at Single Brothers.

So you came in not only to rent a space, but to join the Geneva Two community?

%$#& straight. I had a taste of something and I wanted to drink deeper from that well.

And did you find that deeper drink helpful?

Not in the way I expected. At the time I moved in to Single Brothers, I had this job at the Green Foods market. I came home every day and I was tired and I didn't feel like writing. Basically, I goofed around, writing a little here and a little there, making no progress.

Alan Gasque changed all that. I kept complaining about how my career was stalled and I couldn't even get an agent to return my calls. After a while, Alan had heard enough. He sat me down and said, "Gerry, how much do you write each day?"

"I write when I get the time. It's hard because sometimes I'm in no frame of mind to write."

"But you style yourself a writer…." He said.

"Yeah, I'm a writer."

"Then you're a pretty piss-poor writer, aren't you? What would you do if your doctor cancelled your appointment because he was in no frame of mind to meet with patients?"

I hadn't been to a doctor since I was a kid, but I got his point.

"Listen," he continued, "if you want to be a writer then you need to write every day, whether you feel like it or not. Every day, bang out 5 pages or 3000 words or whatever. You won't get any better unless you practice the discipline of daily practice."

So Alan is a writer too?

No. But he knows human nature. He knew I wouldn't get any better at my art or my life if I didn't learn self-discipline. So he undertook a process of teaching me. It went kind of like this: he yelled at me every morning to make up my bed. I yelled back that he wasn't my mother. Then he'd yell that discipline begins in the small things, and if I wanted to be a writer I'd better learn some discipline or otherwise I'd keep writing crap. It pissed me off, but it made me think. Pretty soon I'd started making my bed every day, first thing after I got up.

And then I noticed that my writing changed. I began to see that by writing daily, I was learning to be a better writer. I still made a $&^* load of mistakes, but I began to see what worked and what didn't work. I started to learn what all this talk about finding a "voice" meant. That first year, I tossed about 85% of everything I wrote, but I also sold a story to *Brave New Worlds* magazine. That gave me hope, you know? I was now a published writer and agents were actually willing to take a look at my work.

And the rest, as they say, is history.

Rosalind Hythloday

Rosalind Hythloday meets me at Ground Up Coffee, where she works part time as a barista and pastry chef. Her other part-time job is working as the "house mother" for the Single Sisters House in the Geneva Two community. She wears the horn-rimmed glasses, skinny jeans, and alternative chic clothing of a modern hipster. A miniscule diamond glitters from the left side of her nose.

I've got to ask – Hythloday is a rather uncommon name. Where's it from?

Ugh! I used to hate my name – can you imagine how much a little girl got teased with such a cumbersome name? "Look there's Rosalind Hit-today!" and then they'd punch me on the arm. High school was worse; the plays on the name became much more profane.

Sorry, I didn't mean to touch a sore spot. It was only idle curiosity.

No, don't worry. I've come to appreciate it now. The family lore says we're descended from wealthy Dutch Traders who founded New Amsterdam.

Quite an illustrious history.

Yeah. But the name is still odd. I'm told that it originally meant "talker of nonsense," so perhaps you shouldn't be wasting your time interviewing me – I'll be loonier than the March Hare.

Not at all. I'm interested in how you came to run the Single Sisters House.

Well, Mathilde Probisco invited me to one of the Sunday evening worship services at their house. Mathilde is a regular here at the shop. She holds a book club here every month, and she also comes by once or twice a week to buy coffee.

Anyway, she was always kind and made the effort to get to know me. We've got a good vibe here at Ground Up – lots of regulars who know each other and use the shop as a meeting place. There's a warmth here that goes a shade or two beyond social nicety. Mathilde is one of those people who keeps pressing your relationship just a bit deeper.

How does she do that?

Mostly by asking good questions – and remembering my answers. Even before she knew me well, she listened to me like she cared. After I told her about the swirling dysfunction of my family (far more than I want to get into here), she remembered names, relationships, and events. She remembered the anniversary of my dad's death and made sure to drop by the shop with a handmade sympathy card. She knew when my roller derby matches were, and she even came to a few.

Wasn't that kind of stalkerish?

Well it sounds like that, I suppose, but really it's the natural way a healthy relationship of any sort develops. It's not like that happened all in one day. Our friendship developed over a couple of years. Just like any friendship, really. You give a little; you listen a lot; you learn.

Of course I enjoyed Mathilde's company – she is one of those people with intellectual heft. Yes, she's an arts-and-crafts, homeschool-mommy kind of person, but she's not the syrupy-sweet, tea-and-crumpets fragile that I expect from that set. I don't feel like I have to guard myself around her. She gives me space to call &^!$#*% and not offend her.

Let me put it another way. A lot of friendships are rooted in competition – sizing yourself up against the other. Sometimes that's a spur to achievement, but many times it's destructive. It's like carving an identity out of somebody else's shortcomings, you know? It's a crazy kind of mentality that says, "So long as I'm surrounded by lesser people, then I can be the alpha dog."

I don't get that feeling from Mathilde. She has no need to be the alpha.

So she invited you to worship. That felt natural?

#@!! No! It was awkward. We'd talked religion before, but inviting someone to worship is like asking a friend out on a date – it's a huge risk. You can imagine all the questions in my mind: What if it's weird? What if they're wack-jobs? Would that wreck the friendship? What if they're a bunch of judgmental jerks? What if it's a cult group?

Did it bother you that it was religious?

No. That wasn't a problem. I know my catechism – I was raised in an old-school Dutch Reformed Church. I probably know more theology than most people in the room. But I was burned out on the institutional church. When Mathilde told me about the house church idea, it really appealed to me. No, religion wasn't the problem – it was the risk to the relationship.

Obviously it worked out.

Yeah, these people are having the kinds of conversations that interest me.

Such as?

What does our faith have to do with how we live? Shouldn't we live differently and share differently? If faith really is about being a new creation, then shouldn't we look demonstrably different? And I don't mean in a weird kind of Stepford difference, but rather in a prophetic critique difference. When Jesus says, "all will know you are my disciples if you love one another," shouldn't that mean something? And if so, then what? Isn't being church something more than being a pawn in some talking head's grand vision? These are the kinds of things that I was interested in talking about, not "five ways to commit to your quiet time."

It sounds like the Single Sisters House arose from those conversations, then?

Alan was seeing some real progress with Single Brothers at the time. A similar house for women seemed like a natural progression. He kept sharing the idea with the community in our weekly prayer time. As we prayed and talked and prayed and talked over the months, it became clear that this was something we should do. A house came open up on the corner of Onieda. Alan put in a bid and got the house. But he needed a house manager to work for him. I felt a real calling to that role, so we worked it out. I get to stay there for free, and in return I manage the house.

Why couldn't he manage it himself?

A guy in his early fifties managing a house for young single women, many of them emotionally vulnerable. Don't you think that sounds just a wee bit creepy?

Yeah. Yeah it does. But there still seem to be possibilities for strangeness in this arrangement.

And there are. One of the things I insisted on is an outside board that oversees both houses – the finances, the leadership, etc. The community prayed over this. We spent time considering who we thought might be good to provide some outside oversight. Now, we've got a five-person board with official incorporation articles and everything. Nathan chairs the board. That helps cut back on the weirdness of it all.

How does that affect the women who live in Single Sisters?

It's mostly invisible to them. I'm their primary contact. I step them through the expectations of living in the house and I mediate most of the disputes. Only if they choose to start worshipping with Geneva Two do they really start to get a sense of the checks and balances in the structure. Of course, right now, all the residents *do* worship at Geneva Two, but that wasn't the case in the early days.

What are some of the challenges you faced in those early days?

The issues that our women brought to the community were completely different from those of the men. Now, I'm painting with a mile-wide paintbrush here, but generally, in Single Brothers House, Alan has to deal with boys who want to be Peter Pan – no commitments, no responsibilities. He has to drill sergeant these boys into taking on responsibility, for the most part.

Generally, in Single Sisters House, we get women who are diligent and responsible, but terribly needy.

What do you mean "needy"?

Well, I've seen it come out in a couple of ways. There are the girls who have no idea of boundaries. They tell people they just met all about their romantic histories and life stories. They share the most awkward and intimate details without any sense of impropriety, and because they expect a "Christian community" to be a certain way, they expect that they'll be loved and embraced. It's hard for girls of this sort to imagine that they come on too strong. When people get freaked out, these girls get sullen and withdrawn.

On the other end of the spectrum there's the fragile person. These girls think they need to work their way into being liked. In return they want the community to tell them what to be. They're so dependent on pleasing someone else that it's like they're chameleons, absorbing their identity from anyone that will pay them mind. The problem always comes when that someone else disappoints. It's amazing how bitter and vindictive they can become. What these girls need is to learn to stand on their own and assert what they are about.

That's a pretty wide range of challenges.

Yes, but at root, the issue is the same: an idolatry of relationship. They think that if they find the right boyfriend or the right set of friends or fix their relationship with their mom, then they will be complete.

It sounds like a recipe for disaster.

It was. That first year was a mess – we brought in three very messy, needy, unstable girls. They nearly chewed one another up before two of them moved out.

From that first experience, we determined to always have at least one stable housemate – preferably someone in the Geneva Two community. It really helps to have one extra calm voice other than mine. When you have a fragile person raging in pain, they need someone safe who can hold them, and then speak calmly as the pain subsides.

Kind of like they were sitting in the ashes with the person who is hurting?

Right. Job's three friends get a bad rap. No one credits them for sitting with Job and letting him groan for days. They may have said some dumb things, but they earned the right to say those dumb things by sitting in the mess with Job.

And remember this, my rant on the neediness of some of our residents is simply my mental digestion of some of those difficult times. Truth be told, we've had stable people come through, too: women who are committed to growth, who are confident in their identity, and know the difference between what they can control and what they can't. Maria Sanchez is a great example – she was with us for a couple of years, and now she's off starting Geneva Farms.

Even so, it sounds like a rough ride for you from time to time.

God has brought me through some hellish experiences. And He's used those experiences to shape me for this job.

Hellish experiences? Can you give me some examples?

Listen, I'm not comfortable sharing any of those stories in an interview that's going in a book. They don't reflect well on me, my family, and others. Suffice it to say that I know rejection and loneliness and judgment and shame. I've looked those demons in the face, and when I did I just crumbled. There, in the midst of mess and insecurity and weeping, Jesus showed up and reminded me that I am not defined by the mess that's happened to me. I'm defined by His gaze and His alone. I'm broken, but I'm not damaged goods. I'm shattered, but whole.

And as you work with these women, you speak to them from your own experience.

When you've been through hell and been brought out on the other side by grace, then you have a deep well from which to draw. I don't wish some of my life experience on anyone. But if I can use it to help bring healing to someone else, I'm in.

Jake Hoffecker

Midway down Amana street, I find the Hoffeckers' well-cared-for house, its trimmed lawn and sculpted shrubbery creating a sense of orderliness. A tight row of border grass lines the perfectly even brick walkway. On the door stoop is a country-style welcome mat decorated with a farm cottage and the message "Welcome Friends." Overall, the home feels homey, comfortable, safe.

Andrea Hoffecker meets me at the door, inviting me in with a cheerful smile. She leads me through a beehive of activity: children playing musical instruments, working on science projects, and reading to one another. Andrea and Jake homeschool their five children, ages 13 down to 3. Somehow, in spite of the swarming preteen energy, they keep the house clean and tidy. In the living room, I find no entertainment center stuffed with electronic gadgetry; rather, I see well-organized bookshelves, neatly arranged musical instruments, and displays of student work.

Andrea ushers me to Jake's downstairs workspace. The finished basement is lined with shelves containing neatly arranged books, videos, and other products of Visionaire House, the publishing and mail order business that Jake runs out of his home.

Jake stands to greet me. He is tall and slender. His sandy blonde hair is cut close, perhaps to mask the extent to which it is receding. With a firm handshake, Jake subtly guides me to a Windsor chair so we can talk.

Thank you for taking the time to talk with me.

Well, thank you for coming to the ogre's den to see the monster.

Ogre's den?

I imagine you've heard some pretty harsh things. I know what people say. I'm this uptight fundamentalist who wants to impose the Christian faith on everyone by force. I'm this angry Pharisee who keeps drawing boxes smaller and smaller. And when I couldn't get my way I took my toys and went home … is that about right?

Perhaps. However, in my experience, no one is ever the villain in their own epic drama.

Epic drama, eh? More like soap opera, I suppose. Anyway, I'm glad that you want to hear my side of things.

So tell me then, why *did* you leave the Geneva Two community?

Jake gives a small sigh. Every group, no matter how small or large, eventually comes to a crisis. It doesn't have to be a bad crisis – success can create a crisis. When a group enjoys success and grows, they discover that they have all these new people who bring different expectations and different understandings. At that point, like it or not, the character of the group has changed.

That's what happened with Geneva Two. When it was only four couples, it was easy. We had already worked through the tough issues, and we had figured out compromises that worked for all of us. Then new people started to join. These people came with different expectations, different ideas. That influx of newness put some serious stress on our understanding of who we were and what our community was about.

Let's just say that when the community grew, it hit a crisis point where they had to define more clearly what they valued. When they settled on a more clear definition, Andrea and I saw that we didn't fit anymore, so we left.

Fair enough. But that's not the full story, is it?

I don't get what you mean.

I don't buy that it was a reasoned, clinical decision. From what I hear, it was a heated fight between you and Alan over the Christian approach to politics.

Alan told you that, did he?

Actually, no.

Probably Hendon, then. He's a great motivational speaker, Hendon is, but he has all the sensitivity of a rusted chainsaw.

So it wasn't politics then?

Oh, Alan and I argued politics, all right. Alan has a gift for toppling straw men rather than dealing with real positions. What he never has been able to grasp is that I'm simply trying to ask good questions – questions that nobody in our world is asking these days.

For example?

You really want to go there?

That's my job.

OK. What happens when our forefathers make covenants of faithfulness with God? What responsibilities do we, as their heirs, have under those covenants? What blessings can we expect? What does it mean that in Genesis, we humans are charged with the responsibility to have dominion over the earth?

I don't hear anyone else asking these questions. People are afraid of the possible answers. They're afraid of sounding too extreme or offending non-Christians and driving them away. It's easier to dismiss the questioner as a nut-job than to give him the respect of actually considering his ideas.

And that's why you left? Because you couldn't persuade Alan and the others to your viewpoint?

Of course not! Even though I had differences with Nathan and Kyle over those ideas all through our early years in Geneva, we never had a problem discussing them with civility and respect. Sane people don't wreck friendships on the rocks of divergent ideas.

So what was it, then? What was it that drove you to leave?

Alan Gasque came in and stole my community away from me. That ... that Svengali, made my best friend choose between me and him.

Tell me more about that.

Alan made it impossible for me to be at peace. From day one, he was questioning the original Geneva Compact. This was what the founders had agreed upon, but it wasn't good enough for Alan. He kept saying it was clumsily worded and it was too narrow and it was a "barrier to recruitment." He insisted that we revise the Compact.

That hurt deeply. I worked really hard on crafting that document, diligently choosing the right words. Not to sound immodest, but I was like the Thomas Jefferson of the group. Everyone had a say in it, but I was the primary author. I put hours of work into honing the Geneva Compact. We had all agreed to it and were building something really beautiful on that foundation.

And then this controlling bully comes along. He doesn't take the time to follow the logic, to understand my reasoning. He launches in with, "It's a good start, but we need to be more realistic on a few points." I ask you, how would Jefferson have reacted to someone saying, "'Life, liberty and the pursuit of happiness,' is a good start, but we need to be more realistic?"

So Alan pushed the revision of the Geneva Compact? That's it?

It is, but it isn't. It's not only that he pushed revision. It's the *way* he pushed it. He never took the time to sit with it and learn the document's virtues. All I wanted was for him to take the time to understand *why* it was written the way it was.

Instead, he immediately began a covert politicking campaign. He'd corner people in a one-on-one setting, then he'd wheedle and cajole them about his concerns with the Compact. Then he would come back to me, saying, "You know, people are talking – there are real concerns about this dominion language...." ARRRGH! That makes me so mad! Whenever someone says, "people are talking," what they mean is, "I've been stirring people up about this." He intentionally went around behind my back, belittling my efforts and work. And he sucked all these people in behind him like children following the pied piper.

So the community as a whole turned against you?

Kind of. I didn't experience any personal attacks or open hostility. But I certainly felt a change in sentiment toward me. It was in the air; people weren't comfortable around me anymore. I was a leper, a pariah.

And that did it? That's why you left?

No. No, it was Nathan.

Nathan? I don't understand.

Losing Nathan's friendship. That broke me.

Broke you? That's a strong statement.

Yeah, it is. But, it's true. Listen, our culture has this peculiar phobia of male friendship. We either dumb it down into a brainless hyper-testosterone, buddy-buddy camaraderie, or we portray male friendship as little more than veiled homo-eroticism – like the campy portrayal of Batman and Robin in the '60s. For some reason, we've lost the ability to talk about male friendship as love in a non-sexual way.

Ok, you need to expand on that a little bit.

The ancient Greeks and Romans talked about friendship in totally different ways than we do. For them, friendship, true friendship, began with the recognition of virtue in the other person. That virtue in the other calls forth the virtue within us. Our true friends make us better, wiser, stronger. It's iron sharpening iron, you know?

What happened to valuing a friend for their character, for their mind, and their worldview? What happened to the idea of seeing the friend as a "second self," as someone whose thoughts and ideas and values echoed my own? These ideals of friendship were understood for centuries, but somehow they've become buried beneath swagger, bluster, and frat-boy shenanigans.

So your relationship with Nathan was different?

He was my best friend. All of us in that early group were close, but Nathan understood where I was coming from better than anyone else. He really listens, and he's fully attentive to whoever he's with. Nathan understood my hopes and dreams, my highest aspirations. In his own way, Nathan is a living embodiment of those dreams.

How do you mean?

My work here, everything I'm doing with Visionaire House, is to provide resources to encourage Christians to reclaim their call to exercise dominion.

Didn't the community reject that idea?

Only as it was caricatured by Alan. Listen, we can talk about theories about "reclaiming America" and "dominon over the earth" – but those are all far off possibilities that will never be realized in this generation.

I'm planting seeds. Before we can change the world, we first need to learn to exercise dominion in the small things. We need to run our homes like little islands of sanity in the seas of chaos of the world. We need communities of healthy sharing and Christian discipleship – new monastic communities if you will. Isn't that what you've experienced at Geneva Two?

Well yes…

And we need to start businesses, small family-run businesses. Businesses that are blessings to the community and managed according to godly principles. Isn't that what Nathan is doing at Poiema?

Why sure …

You see? Alan may reject the language of dominion – he may have persuaded the people of Geneva Two that my understanding of community accountability is cult-like. Even so, they're exercising dominion over what God has entrusted *to them*. They're not passively accepting the dysfunctional offerings of the world. All of them, even Alan, I have to grudgingly admit, are trying to rebuild the ruins of our culture.

And all of that continues to happen because Nathan, deep in his core, is on the same page with me.

Yet you say your relationship with him is broken?

Alan turned him against me. Wait, that's too strong. I really don't think Nathan is against *me*. But Alan pushed the dominion issue and the revisions to the compact. Like I said, in the end Nathan felt pressured to choose between me and Alan.

And Alan won.

Basically. I can't fault Nathan. Alan was his high school teacher, after all. Alan has known Nathan far longer than I have. And Nathan is one of those peacemakers – he's able to maintain friendships with vastly different people. I guess he felt caught between two mighty forces, and eventually he had to break and take a side.

Two mighty forces. That implies that you were matching Alan's pushiness.

Pause. Yeah. To be honest, I really wasn't at my best. When I'm pushed, I fight. Alan pushed hard, so I fought back.

And was the fight worth it?

Pause again. No one's ever asked me that. I was standing for what I know to be right – so that was worth it. But if I knew then what it would cost in terms of broken relationships … well … I might've approached the situation differently.

So now you're estranged from the community … how do you handle that?

I pray. I pray a lot for the people that I'm estranged from. Jesus says to love your enemies and pray for those who persecute you. For quite a while, my anger burned against Alan and, truth be told, Nathan. God made it really clear to me that I had to release that anger. So when they came to mind and I found my anger simmering, I prayed for them.

What were those prayers like?

At first I spent a lot of time telling God how angry I was. The Psalms show us we can be bold in expressing our feelings – our anger, our sorrow, our despair – directly to God. It was a really strange experience. I was reading the imprecatory psalms – the ones that talk about God destroying your enemies.

Rather disturbing parts of the Bible, don't you think?

You know, those psalms are disturbing, but they're not about us taking vengeance in our own hands. They're about committing our cause to God and crying out for justice.

They're still disturbing.

OK, OK, but follow along with me for a moment. As I prayed through those psalms, I came to some powerful realizations. First, I realized that I didn't really want that kind of punishment for Alan. I was angry with him, but I didn't want him destroyed.

That's comforting.

Second, I realized that I didn't really want justice either. If I'm a sinner, then I deserve the same kind of destruction described in those imprecatory psalms. It would be hypocritical for me to cry out for justice to be applied to others when I am in deep need of mercy myself.

And that's when I realized that the wrath of God described in those psalms is the same wrath that Christ suffered on the cross. That's where God's justice is made perfect: in the mercy Jesus shows on the cross.

You arrived at mercy from the imprecatory psalms?

And from Jesus' own words. He said, "*Love your enemies* and pray for those who persecute you." I learned that God knows a lot better than I do what Alan Gasque needs and how to work on him. God is fully aware of Alan's sin, but also fully aware of my own. And one thing is true: Alan and I both need mercy.

So then I started to pray through different scriptures. I turn to the end of Galatians and pray that God would help Alan grow in the fruit of the Spirit: love, joy, peace, patience, kindness, goodness, faithfulness, gentleness, and self-control. I turn to Ephesians and pray that God would give Alan the power to grasp the height, the depth, the breadth, and the width of God's love expressed to him in Christ Jesus.

God has been teaching me that to "pray for those who persecute you," means to pray for God's greatest blessings to be manifest in their lives. If they are growing deeper in Christ and His grace, and if I am growing deeper in Christ and His grace, then eventually, we will have some form of reconciliation. Even if it isn't in this lifetime.

And clearly it hasn't happened yet.

No it hasn't. I've still got some hurt to release. And God's not done with me yet.

Nathan Probisco

You've had quite the interesting ride these past 10 years. Starting a business, a family, and an intentional community.

It's been quite the adventure. You know, the only one of those that I had planned for was the family. The business and the community just seemed to happen; they certainly weren't pieces of any master plan on my part. We just kept taking what seemed like the next step, and then another step. And before we knew it – here we are.

You know, people around here love you a lot. I've observed that in many ways you're the heart and soul of this community.

That's very kind. I don't know about that, though …

Just take it for granted. As you look back over the past decade of Geneva Two, what has stood out for you?

I never expected that our little small group would become a model for Christian community. I keep thinking about what Paul says in Romans 8: "In all things, God works to the good for those who love him and are called according to his purpose." It's been a good ten years. But I must admit, it has also been a hard, painful ten years.

That is not what I expected to hear at all...

Really? The fallout between Jake and Alan broke my heart. They were two of my best friends. Admittedly, they were friends from different eras of my life, but still I consider them both to be people I love and would sacrifice for. Jake helped found the community; Alan came in later, but brought a real creativity and vitality. Both poured heart and soul into making this community special. When Jake left, even though he said it had nothing to do with me, I felt crushed.

But the Hoffeckers still live right around the corner...

Which makes it even harder. Even though they're there, it's not the same. We don't share the same events and activities anymore. We live in parallel universes, in a way. So when we do see each other and talk, we awkwardly dance about, grasping for words. It's the constant visible reminder of a failure of community. I ache over that.

Does that, in a sense, invalidate what you're trying to do?

I don't know I would say it invalidates it. You've been around us – we're not Utopians here. We don't claim that somehow we're offering a flawless community. We're honest that we are a bunch of sinful people. Conflict is bound to happen and people are bound to leave. Most of the time, we handle it pretty maturely, but it still hurts when it happens. Our honesty about the dark things in life doesn't take away the pain, but our honesty does push us to rely on God's grace. Ultimately, grace trumps pain. The dark things, though they still hurt, cease to define us.

But I tell you, my pain isn't only from the conflict. I'm a sentimental softie. Every time someone leaves the community, even for good and exciting reasons, I ache inside.

Every time? Even with the offshoot communities you're establishing downtown and at Geneva Farm?

Yes, every time. Don't get me wrong, it's a mixed feeling. It's wonderful that our way of living inspires our people to replicate it in different places. But, when they leave, it's still a change in relationship. I can delight in what you're going to do and still be sad that you won't be close anymore.

But that's life, isn't it? Children grow up and move out of the house. Beloved mentors retire from the workplace. People we love pass away. You can't be consumed with sadness when these changes happen.

Ah, I never said I was consumed. I said I was sad and it was painful. That's just the point I was making earlier about grace trumping pain. We have this idolatrous idea that life should be devoid of pain. When painful life transitions happen, we run from the pain. We numb it with any number of addictions. Or, if we think we are very strong, we try to grit our teeth and deny that the pain has any reality. None of these approaches are healthy.

It reflects poorly upon my relationships if a change in those relationships doesn't affect me. I give my friends no credit if I don't mourn their moving away. Every goodbye is a little preparation for death, and it hurts. Feeling the pain of change gives testimony that my friends are valuable and they have blessed me. No – I face the pain, but I'm not consumed by it, at least not on my better days.

But won't that crush you, after a while?

It would, if I were alone. Go back to that verse I mentioned earlier – God works all things to the good for those who love him. My friends move on; it hurts. But I trust that God has plans for them. I pray for them, wish them well, and thank God for the time we've had.

Sure, there are times when I wallow in emotional pain, churning the past over and over in the mind, replaying the movie of past events in my head. Or fantasizing, reliving past glories. These are all passive solitary activities, and when I do these things, the pain gets the better of me.

Yet God has this way of breaking through like a ray of light through a bank of clouds. When I wallow in my sadness, He calls me to prayer. He calls me to give a name to the present feeling, commit it to Him, and then move on.

It's strange. By embracing the pain, I'm able to leave it behind. God makes it a part of me, but he blunts the cutting edge of the hurt. The pain makes me stronger – like melting two metals together to make a stronger alloy. Like how certain chemicals combine to make a stronger bonding agent. By itself, quicklime burns. But quicklime with sand and water makes pretty good concrete.

What doesn't kill you makes you stronger, eh?

Not quite. Don't forget the critical component … the work of God in the heart. Without God's work in my heart, the pain can harden into a crusty shell. It can calcify into a barrier. Left to my own devices, I would take that pain and become a cranky, bitter person. But God uses the pain to make me soft and tender. God pushes me to keep risking myself in relationships with people. And He keeps giving me the strength to do so.

And so ….

And so, I can rejoice in what God is doing through those who have left the community. I can praise God because Jake's business is encouraging homeschoolers across the country. I can praise God that what was once Trinity Presbyterian is now reaching hundreds more people with the Grace of Christ. I can praise God that a cluster of people is moving into Over-the-Rhine. I can praise God that another cluster is moving out to farmland of rural Butler County. I can rejoice in all these people who are discovering God's calling on their lives – even if I am no longer in a position to directly encourage them in their callings.

I guess God has given me a glimpse of how, through His providence, our actions ripple far beyond what we can expect. And in that, I am happy.

And what about you … what does the future hold for you?

We have children. We have a community. We have a vocation. These are plenty to keep me occupied for the next ten years and many more beyond.

**But what about vision? You are something of a
community leader, you know. Now that you've tasted
success with the community, what are the visions for the
next phase?**

Laughs. I'll leave the vision casting and the big ideas to the
institutions. We're a community here, not an institution.
Institutions have their place in the world – they are cultural arks.
They are the vehicles of transmission of culture from one
generation to the next. Institutional churches are necessary; they
gather people together and become incubators for ministry ideas.
Don't forget that Geneva Two would never have happened
without the earlier nurture of the institutional church. We need
large institutions to be a repository of learning for the Body of
Christ.

But our little community – it's not an institution. Not
everyone needs to supply a grand overarching dream. Sometimes,
it is enough to steward the little bit that God has entrusted to you.

No. I am content. Paul says it, and I say it too. I've learned
the secret of being content in all things, whether in plenty or in
poverty – I can do all things through Christ who strengthens me.

From Hatcher's Files: An Email from Jake Hoffecker

To: hchristolphson@gimletmedia.com
From: dominionjake@entmail.com
RE: Interview

Mr. Christolphson, thank you for interviewing me RE Geneva Two. I appreciate your commitment to getting the full story and giving me the chance to tell my part of the tale.

After our interview, I was agitated for the rest of the day. Our conversation kept replaying in my head. I was struck by the incongruity between my lingering anger with Alan and my high-minded words about prayer.

I've spent the last few days examining the state of my heart, and I've not been encouraged with what I've found.

This morning, I was reading Matthew 5 for my morning prayers. That's the part that includes the instruction that if you are offering a gift at the altar and you remember that your brother has anything against you, then you should go and be reconciled first.

I have read those words countless times. But this morning, I felt God pressing them onto my conscience.

I can only count it an act of God's providence that brought you into my life at just this time. Your careful interview was His instrument to lead me to re-evaluate some of the choices I've made in my relationships.

I want you to know that I've just come from Alan Gasque – I called him immediately after my morning prayers and set up some time to see him.   I confessed to him my ill will and bad feelings. I told him that even though I haven't changed my position about the Christian's role in society, I have repented of how I handled our conflict over that position.   I sought his forgiveness, and he granted it.   We will likely never be friends.   But we have at least ended the feud.   I still have yet to talk with Nathan, but I anticipate that conversation will be far easier.

I wanted you to know these things.   Whatever comes of your project, please know that it has resulted in good.   I do believe that in any given encounter, God is up to far more things than we can be aware of.   Eternity will tell the full results of your work in capturing some of the Geneva Two story.   However I wanted you to know one small immediate benefit, in hopes that it might encourage you.

May God bless you in your work.

Jake Hoffecker

From Hatcher's Files: An Email from Nathan Probisco

To: hchristolphson@gimletmedia.com
From: nprobisco@poiemafurnishings.org
RE: Jake and Alan

Hatcher,

Yes, I did hear about it. Jake called me this afternoon, probably shortly after he sent you his message.

I've been crying. Tears of joy.

God is good.

Nathan

Acknowledgements

I'm deeply grateful to all my friends who have patiently listened to me prattle on about *Geneva Two*. If I have learned anything about community, I have learned it through those who care for and encourage me.

I received valuable feedback from many early readers: Rod Ford, Smythe Kannapell, Ed Eubanks, Adam Tisdale, Sherri Ellington, Rob and Genita Heidenreich, Robert Burns, Kathy Callahan-Howell, and Michael Card.

Jodi Craiglow and Sherri Ellington provided detailed editorial readings. Their questions, suggestions, and insights vastly improved the manuscript.

Over the past four years, I've benefitted from the support, wisdom, and counsel of a great pastor's prayer group: Tom Sweets, Jeff Hosmer, Erwin Goedicke, Alan Landes, and Tim McQuade.

The good people of Covenant-First Presbyterian Church have been invaluable in helping me shape my ideas. I'm thankful for all our members and our "extended family" of people who are connected to the church in some way.

Mom and Dad have always been my biggest cheerleaders, and they have continued to have unflagging zeal for this project. I am forever grateful for all the opportunities they have given me and the ways they have shaped me.

My siblings, Jack Smith and Dr. Alison T. Smith, have always encouraged me in so many ways – the benefit of being the youngest, I suppose.

Sarah Grace and Annalise Smith bring me delight and joy, more than I'm capable of expressing.

And Tammy Smith, my wife, my friend, my advisor, my support, and my muse. Thank you for forging a home with me.

Finally, a word of thanks to Christ, the living Word. While I claim no special inspiration for this text, I most certainly would never have written this without Christ's ongoing work and presence in my life. Soli Deo Gloria!

About the Author

Russell B. Smith graduated with a degree in English Literature from Wake Forest University. After four years in the corporate world as a technical trainer, he pursued a call to ordained ministry. He received his Masters of Divinity from Reformed Theological Seminary in Orlando, and since 2001 has served as Senior Pastor of Covenant-First Presbyterian Church in Cincinnati, OH (www.covfirstchurch.org). Many members of the congregation have contributed to this work through their encouragement and thoughtful reading of early manuscripts.

Russell holds a Masters Degree in Ancient Cultures from the University of Stellenbosch. In his spare time, he enjoys cooking, reading, and dragging his family to every museum or cultural attraction he can find. He and his wife Tammy take great joy in helping their daughters grow into all God has called them to be.

Russell has written one other book, the action adventure novel *Prophet of the Sun*. He has also contributed to *Send Me: The Story of Salkehatchie Summer Service*. His 2013 white paper "Ministry in the Age of Design" was called a 'must read' and is available for free on the Horizons of the Possible blog.

Follow Russell on social media:

- Twitter: @possiblehorizon
- Instagram: @possiblehorizon
- Blog: www.horizonsofthepossible.wordpress.com

Made in the USA
Middletown, DE
05 December 2014